THE GHOST DETECTIVES'

GUIDE TO HAUNTED SAN FRANCISCO

Loyd Auerbach & Annette Martin

CRAVEN STREET

B O O K S

Fresno, California

map provided by Pat Hunter, Gallery II
cover photograph © Stephen Coburn - Fotolia.com
all photos by the authors unless otherwise noted

Published by Craven Street Books
an imprint of Linden Publishing
2006 South Mary, Fresno, California 93721
559-233-6633 / 800-345-4447
QuillDriverBooks.com

Craven Street Books and Colophon are trademarks of
Linden Publishing, Inc.

ISBN 978-1-610350-07-5

135798642

Printed in the United States of America
on acid-free paper.

Library of Congress Cataloging-in-Publication Data

Auerbach, Loyd.
The ghost detectives guide to haunted San Francisco / Loyd Auerbach &
Annette Martin.
    p. cm.
Includes bibliographical references and index.
ISBN 978-1-61035-007-5 (pbk. : alk. paper)
1. Haunted places--California--San Francisco. 2. Ghosts--California--San
Francisco. 3. Ghosts--Research--Methodology. I. Martin, Annette. II. Title.
BF1472.U6A94 2011
133.109794'61--dc22
                            2010051696

Praise for
The Ghost Detectives'
Guide to Haunted San Francisco

"An honest and top quality work which will delight those wanting a spooky ghost book, and, at the same time, please those seasoned readers of the paranormal who wish a book that delivers valuable research and seeks seriously to answer the eternal question that perplexes all of us: If a ghost was once a person like us, then are we all potential ghosts?"
—from the foreword by **Brad Steiger**, author of *Real Ghosts, Restless Spirits and Haunted Places*

"A delightful book that is a must-have handbook for everyone and anyone thinking of investigating the best haunts in historical San Francisco. Don't go there without reading this first!"
—**Chris Fleming**, sensitive, paranormal investigator and co-host of *Dead Famous* on the Biography Channel and A&E's *Psychic Kids*

"Should you plan on visiting and investigating the Bay Area, I highly suggest reading *The Ghost Detectives' Guide to Haunted San Francisco* before you do."
—**Chad Calek**, paranormal investigator featured on A&E's *Paranormal State* and *The Ghost Prophecies* and director of *American Ghost Hunter*

"San Francisco is haunted! Loyd Auerbach and Annette Martin offer an inspiring and at times chilling tour of the city by the Bay. Great book!"
—**Jeff Belanger**, writer and researcher of the Travel Channel's *Ghost Adventures* series

"Annette Martin blows me away. She is the real thing. She not only sees the dead but speaks to them, gets them to let down their guard and tell us their secrets. I have never seen anything like it!"
—**Lydia Cornell**, star of *Too Close for Comfort* and *Curb Your Enthusiasm*

"Another paranormal gem from the well-known and respected field investigator and paranormal educator Loyd Auerbach, as he reviews the investigations of several favorite San Francisco sites conducted with his long-time colleague Annette Martin."
—**Sally Rhine Feather**, director, Rhine Research Center

CONTENTS

Foreword

If we may assume from the evidence of prehistoric burial sites that our species has pondered the mystery of life after death for about 60,000 years, it seems likely that humankind has been recounting the appearances of ghosts for at least that long. During that expanse of time there have always been shamans and mystics who have deliberately sought to contact the spirits of the deceased. However, in the conventional ghost report it is a specter that manifests to frighten or to enlighten the surprised beholder. Never, until the past few years, have there been legions of humans who have sought out haunted places so that they might hunt ghosts.

Yes, there was the rise of Spiritualism in the United States in the 1850s that, according to some historians, brought as many as eleven million believers to the séance table or spirit circle. When we consider that the population of the U.S. at that period in our history was approximately 30 million, the acceptance of Spiritualism as a religion served a sizeable percentage of the nation. When Spiritualism began to fade as a movement in the 1870s, such groups as the British Society for Psychical Research, founded in 1882, undertook a serious study of mediumship, apparitions, séances, and haunted houses.

Until quite recently, haunted houses and things that go bump in the night have remained the province of laboratory researchers and a few individuals who, because of their interest in ghosts or because of their demonstrated mediumship abilities, were called upon to investigate places thought to be haunted.

However, today, "ghost busters" and "ghost hunters" abound on cable television and radio programs. It now seems as if every village with a population of over 1,000 has a ghost hunting group. Indeed, some of these individuals with a self-professed ability to ferret out ghosts may have some right to claim such an ephemeral talent. In far too many instances, however, the credentials of the "ghost busters" consists only of watching the aforementioned cable programs and in some rare cases actually reading a few books on the subject.

How wonderfully refreshing it is to discover two highly qualified "ghost detectives" who have given of their unique talents to present a guide to haunted places in various cities, beginning with some of the well-known sites in San Francisco. I have known and respected the skills and acumen of parapsychological field researcher Loyd Auerbach for many years, and in the past three years I have come to delight in the multi-level paranormal abilities of Annette Martin, who surely ranks as one of the top psychic sensitives in the United States today.

Annette has been psychically gifted since she was a child of seven and has shared her gifts with hundreds of individuals, as well as assisting the police in recent years as a psychic detective. Annette is also a gifted singer, having her own radio program when she was ten and going on to sing with many opera companies. I have theorized that psychic ability is a talent given to certain individuals and if that person did not become a psychic, he or she might display a gift for painting, writing, dancing, and so forth. Annette proves the theory many times over, expressing her creativity in so many areas.

Loyd is my kind of psychic investigator. He doesn't load himself down with a lot of fancy high-tech gadgets that, in my opinion, more often than not merely provide environmental static that less astute researchers interpret as genuine indications of actual ghost phenomena. Loyd is open to many sources of information that may be present in a genuine haunting—primary in this book to be that provided through the mediumship of Annette Martin. Loyd is constantly evaluating whatever input seems relevant, rejecting—or at least tabling—that which seems extraneous to the case.

Annette and Loyd have chosen to express this book largely in the form of a dialog between them as they investigate a haunting. This technique allows the readers to feel that they are actually participating in the investigation as it progresses at each location. Historical background and other research elements are also provided to allow readers a total immersion in each case.

I spoke to Annette before they investigated the many ghosts of San Francisco's Chinatown, and I advised her that August, the month they had chosen to visit the sites, was the "Month of Hungry Ghosts" in the Chinese tradition. She answered with a laugh that she was well aware of that fact, and she promised to come back with lots of good stories. Readers may discover for themselves that Annette fulfilled her promise.

On the Jeff Rense Program just before Halloween a few years back, we conducted a live radio broadcast from the Moss Beach Distillery Restaurant with Annette, Loyd, and the ghostly Blue Lady herself. It was chillingly fascinating to hear Annette conversing with this charming ghost, who doesn't wish to leave the picturesque location by the ocean. The Blue Lady also seems to have a kind of spirited crush on Loyd.

This is a book that readers may explore with full confidence. Loyd and Annette deliver an honest and top quality work which will delight those wanting a spooky ghost book, and, at the same time, please those seasoned readers of the paranormal who wish a book that delivers valuable research and seeks seriously to answer the eternal question that perplexes all of us: If a ghost was once a person like us, then are we all potential ghosts?

Brad Steiger, author of
Real Ghosts, Restless Spirits, and Haunted Places

Introduction

Do you like a good ghost story?

Are you a paranormal tourist, someone who likes to visit places with reported haunting and other unexplained activity?

Or are you a ghost hunter/paranormal investigator looking for ghosts in all the right places?

If you fall into any or all of the above categories, you've probably purchased (or borrowed) books that list haunted places in a given town, county, or state—or even one of the national or international directories.

These books can be very helpful, but most of them simply repeat short descriptions of what has been reported before—often years before. Some few provide longer tales of the location, the author having done some research on the history and on rare occasions including quotes from actual witnesses. There may be references to what a psychic or medium may have "picked up" in the place and even occasional references to communication with the resident spirits.

This book is in a different class all together.

Our intention is to give you more than what you've ever gotten when reading about a haunted location and to focus on quality of information, not quantity of locations. You'll get the story from a very different set of perspectives: a professional psychic/medium and a professional parapsychologist.

I am that parapsychologist, someone who studies psychic phenomena. I've been reading about and studying psychic experiences since well before I entered grad school in 1979 to gain my master's degree in parapsychology.

I am a generalist in the field and an educator, teaching classes locally and via distance learning, and lecturing about different aspects of parapsychological studies from ESP to investigating apparitional cases.

I am also a parapsychological field researcher. I used to use the terms "ghost hunter" and "paranormal investigator," but they've been co-opted by ever-growing armies of amateur and hobbyist folks.

In reality, what we do as field researchers or investigators is much more like what a detective or investigative journalist does. We try to solve mysteries, find out whodunit (and who they are or were) and why, and help with resolutions where applicable.

In parapsychological field investigations of the type discussed in this book, we look at those psychic phenomena and experiences that have been called *ghostly*, for which we use terms like apparition, haunting and poltergeist. Contrary to what you might see on ghost hunter websites, all of these phenomena are "of the mind," whether that mind be living or dead, and therefore psychic by definition. Too many make the mistake of using *psychic* when referring to what a psychic or medium is doing, as opposed to the phenomena itself. The term most often used—paranormal—really can be applied to a much broader range of reported phenomena and experiences that are currently unexplained by science, and considered *on the side of normal,* which is what paranormal means. Many consider UFO and Bigfoot sightings paranormal, but such things are not related to psychic phenomena other than by their currently unexplained nature.

For purposes of familiarity, we'll use the terms psychic and paranormal interchangeably, but we'd like our readers to always remember that such things are part of the continuum of psychic phenomena studied by parapsychologists.

In public venues such as those you'll read about in this book (and hopefully visit), we first try to determine if there is anything psychic happening *still.* All too often, the places listed in the various books and directories may at one time have been haunted, but are no longer.

To start, we rely heavily on recent reports of people having witnessed or experienced something at the locations. Without current reports, there's really nothing to indicate that the place is or is not still active.

Once we determine the possible continuation of the phenomena and consider more normal explanations, we look into the reported phenomena with all the tools of our arsenal: interviewing skills (to work further with witnesses), environmental sensors, and psychics and mediums.

While amateurs and hobbyists rely foremost on their devices—equipment which has not been proven to detect anything paranormal—

what that technology can show at best is that there are anomalies in the environment. Unexplained electromagnetic fields do not in and of themselves indicate a ghost, and odd images on a thermalvision camera do not mean there's an entity present. Without something to connect the odd readings to (after all other explanations have been exhausted), all you have is odd readings.

To give meaning to the anomalies picked up by technology, you need a person or people to experience the events. After all, it is those person-based experiences which actually define the phenomena. Kind of like the old question, "If a tree falls in the woods, and no one is around to hear it, does it make a noise?" According to physics, it makes a sound but noise is a qualitative label that requires an observer.

It is interesting to note, where there is a ghost, that ghost *was a person.* In other words, people are involved in apparition cases even when there are no living people present. Real people left the impressions in residual hauntings when they were alive.

I've worked with different "human detectors" over the years. Some have identified their abilities early in life, and learned to understand and apply them to various practices (psychics and mediums). Some were simply people who had a real encounter in the past in cases that I've investigated.

Unlike a piece of high-tech equipment, I can ask these detectors questions in an attempt to identify whatever it is the witnesses are experiencing. Does the situation indicate a conscious entity—an apparition or spirit—or an imprint of a past event or person—essentially a recording?

While some people have used Electronic Voice Phenomena (EVP) and various meters to attempt communication (not much different than the much-maligned Ouija board), direct communication between the human detectors and conscious beings or apparitions, if present, provides a better understanding of who might be present, why they're present, and what they need from us living folk.

There's a ghost story which brings in the ghost detectives, there's the evidence gathering and interviewing of witnesses, and there's the information psychic consultants pick up from the environment and/or the disembodied "clients."

In this book, you'll get more than the story. You'll get the actual impressions and communications perceived by a top psi (psychic) operative, Annette Martin, and a parapsychologist's reaction to that and other evidence gathered. We'll be giving you an idea of what it's like to look in depth into a haunted location, from the view of a scientist and a psychic.

The style of these presentations varies from transcript to narrative. We do this to do best justice to the locations and our visits.

Annette and I intend this book to be the first of a series. Each will take a region, at first in and around the greater Bay Area in Northern California. Each will give you a psychic's take on a still-active location. We're starting in our own near-and-dear backyard, though we certainly plan to go well beyond, in more ways than one.

May the Force be with you,
Loyd Auerbach

****

B eing a medical intuitive at age seven, seeing and talking to ghosts as a child, and working as a professional psychic detective for the past forty years has been quite an awesome adventure.

I have the great honor of having received world-wide exposure for my police investigations and ghost detective work, including appearances on: *Good Morning America*, Court TV's *Psychic Detectives*, the BBC, *Entertainment Tonight, Coast to Coast Radio* show, *The Nancy Grace Show, Catherine Crier Show, 48 Hours*, ABC, The Discovery Channel, The History Channel, The Travel Channel, CBS News, *The Montel Williams Show* and numerous other national and international television shows. They call me the "Radio Psychic," due to my being the hostess of the first psychic radio talk show in 1976, and I have been a featured guest on hundreds of radio programs in the U.S. and abroad.

At age ten I became a professional singer, which has carried through to today. I have had the opportunity to sing with many opera companies around the world, including San Francisco & Los Angeles Civic Light Opera Co. and Belles Artes Opera Company in Mexico City.

When Loyd Auerbach asked me to join him in 1994 at the Moss Beach Distillery to contact a very active ghost known as The Blue Lady, I was thrilled. Our encounter with each other went very well and since that time I have accompanied Loyd on numerous investigations.

We definitely make a good team, and we have come to see ourselves as "ghost detectives," who search out and discover clues to the presence of an

energy that is the consciousness after the death of the body, a consciousness that has not moved on to what I call the White Light (also referred to
as the "Other Side" by many).

In many cases, folks think that they have a ghost, but it frequently
turns out that it is a residual impression or residual haunting that they are
encountering.

These residual hauntings are like videos that play over and over and are
generally stuck in one place. An intense emotion, such as one originating
during a murder or a fight or stemming from a great fear, may leave an
impression or recording in its surroundings. The impression can originate
from a very positive but emotional event as well.

The replay of such a recording can then, somehow, be triggered, acting
as a "telepathic virtual reality show." This of course can happen in a home,
a hotel, a restaurant, or another building—even in a cemetery.

Because, as mentioned above, it is like a closed video loop, you cannot
communicate or interact with a residual haunting.

When Loyd and I enter a site, I can immediately identify the difference
between an actual ghost or a residual haunting. With ghosts, the first thing
that happens is that I get goose bumps all over my body, a signal that we
have a consciousness nearby.

The ghosts will then come over to me, showing himself (or herself)—
either quite solidly from head to legs or with the body portion a bit trans-
parent. The ghost will generally begin by asking me, "Who are you?" I will
engage him in conversation, identifying myself and asking him who he is
and why he's present.

Throughout the years I have found that during this conversation I am
actually counseling the ghosts about the lives that they led on earth and
what they are doing as a ghost. Many have wanted help with moving into
the Light, but then there are many who, for various reasons, have chosen
to stay here on Earth. It has always been our practice to never force a
consciousness to leave, especially if they are frightened or confused about
going to the Light.

We often are able to gather a great deal of evidence about ghosts by
researching historical records and interviewing people who have had
similar experiences at the site. Through this research we have frequently
obtained confirmation of what we have found, adding validity to our investigations. Because of this, many questions have been answered and many
cases solved.

In the process, we also often help the people who live or work in the
home or other location deal with their experiences.

I hope that you will enjoy our adventures in and around San Francisco, my city-by-the-Bay. We want to share with you a better perception of this invisible world around us, helping you to a fear-free understanding that will help you to integrate and soothe your consciousness to a higher level.

May the White Light be with you,
Annette Martin

"What Are Ghosts?" and Other Questions

We thought we'd start out by answering a few questions about the paranormal phenomena we'll be discussing throughout this book and to place it in some sort of context. Not meant to be the be-all-end-all for questions and answers, think of this as your entry point to our perspective, giving you an idea of what parapsychologists think ghosts and the like really are, and how these apparitions tie into other psychic experiences. We've decided to do this in a Q&A fashion, as we thought you'd find it more interesting that way.

What Is a Ghost?

The term "ghost" has covered a variety of experiences in many cultures. In general most people use "ghost" to mean a spirit or other form of a person after he or she has died. However, the word is also sometimes applied to any figure of a person or animal experienced in any location where the person or animal is not really there, especially when the ghost represents someone or some animal that has died.

There's often no distinction made as to whether the ghost is a conscious being or just some kind of recording of a person, animal, or event. Parapsychologists do make the distinction and often use the term "apparition" to refer to the concept of a human personality or consciousness (or that of an animal) appearing in some form after death.

Annette Martin and other psychics/mediums will often make a distinction between a disembodied consciousness that has not moved beyond the Earth and ones that have moved on but are back, often communicating from the "Light" or "other side" through a medium. Annette uses "ghost" or "apparition" to refer to the earthbound folks, and "spirit" to refer to those who have moved into the Light. The cases in this book, when dealing with disembodied consciousness, are mainly those of ghosts or apparitions.

There are other categories for similar—but different—experiences.

What are those categories?

The "big three" which we investigate are apparitions, hauntings, and poltergeists. In shortened form, they are disembodied (after death) consciousnesses, recordings or "impressions," and living-agent psychokinesis. With the first, we'll use the terms "apparitions" and "ghosts" interchangeably.

The second events are generally called "hauntings," though Annette and many other psychics use the term "residual hauntings" to make it clear that a deceased entity is not involved.

The poltergeist case—something that includes significant object movement and breakage in a chaotic fashion—has for decades been defined by parapsychologists as quite different from cases of ghosts moving objects. In the former, there's much destruction and chaos which symbolizes a *living person's unconscious* using psychokinesis (PK), also known as "mind over matter," to blow off steam. In the latter, the ghost is usually using psychokinesis to move objects in an attention-getting or even fun-loving, mischief-producing way.

Tell us more about apparitions...

An apparition, a.k.a. "ghost," is the personality (or consciousness, or mind, or whatever you want to call it) surviving the death of the body that is capable of *interaction* with the living (and presumably other such disembodied folks). It is pure consciousness. Apparitions are seen, heard, felt, or smelled (thankfully, not tasted!) by people through the process of *telepathic* communication.

The model of an apparition is that it is consciousness without form. As the ghost has no form, and no sensory organs or normal ability to communicate, he or she essentially connects to the minds of living people. The ghost basically broadcasts sensory information (what he or she looks, sounds, feels, and/or smells like) to the minds of us living folk. The brain or consciousness (it's unclear whether it's one, the other, or both) processes the signals and add them to what our normal senses are picking up. Some people do this better with visual input, some with auditory or other kind of sensory input. Some, like Annette Martin, can process combinations easily.

But because they have no physical form, ghosts are not seen with the eye or heard with the ear. That's why, in a crowded room with lots of living people and a ghost, some see the ghost, some hear him, some feel his presence, some smell his cologne and some get different combinations of these perceptions. And of course, many people in the room may get nothing at all. This is also why ghosts can't be photographed—they don't reflect light.

But aren't there photos of ghosts?

There are many—too many—pictures out there of various light shapes that people have concluded are ghosts and spirits, generally without exploring other photographic reasons why the light appears in the picture. Two main photo issues account for the vast majority of observed orbs and other shapes:

1. Reflections of the flash or the infra-red light used to help a camera focus. Just because you can't see an obviously reflective surface in the frame of the photo doesn't mean there wasn't one in range of the flash or infra-red. Dust does not need to be in sight; it can be less than an inch from the lens and still reflect the flash.
2. With digital cameras, there are often "drop-outs" of individual or small groups of pixels that get converted to "orbs" when the picture goes from the digital data to what we see as the image.

If ghosts could appear in a picture, it would be because they consciously affected the film or digital media, not because they simply appear in a bright flash (which is absolutely not the case). In other words, the apparition affects the picture media with his or her mind. By definition, this is a form of psychokinesis or mind over matter.

Is that how ghosts also move objects?

Yes. If a ghost causes an object to move, it's by PK at its purest form: pure mind affecting matter.

Of course, living people can also do this.

So a ghost photo could be caused by a living person's PK?

Yes. The expectations and desires of the photographer or someone else present, directed at actually capturing something on camera, could trigger an unconscious burst of PK that affects the film or digital media.

So people can cause things to move or otherwise affect things mentally? Is that what a poltergeist is?

The term poltergeist can be traced back hundreds of years, but has come to represent something very different than the literal translation of the German word for "noisy ghost." In poltergeist cases, physical effects are the central theme, including movements and levitations, the appearance or disappearance of objects, unusual behavior of electrical appliances, unexplained knockings or other sounds, and temperature changes. Combinations of these are possible as well. Rarely are ghostly figures or voices seen or heard.

The model we work from is called *recurrent spontaneous psychokinesis*, or RSPK. It is PK that happens without conscious control, and happens over and over. It doesn't come from an apparition or ghost, but from someone living or working in the environment where the poltergeist outbreak is happening.

What about your other category, residual hauntings?

Like the poltergeist, a residual haunting relies on the living. Unlike a poltergeist case, where the phenomena are *caused* by the agent, the impression in a residual haunting is *received* by people. Such hauntings actually show that we are all psychic receivers (clairvoyant) to some degree.

Ever walk into a house and get a feel for the "vibes"—the house feels "good" or "bad"? Of course, that feeling could be because of normal perceptions—the décor is perhaps to your liking, or not—but you may be also psychically perceiving emotions and events—impressions—embedded in the environment.

One ability proffered by many psychics over the ages is psychometry: the ability to "read" the history of an object by holding or touching it. Objects, we're told, "record" their entire history, and some can decipher that with psi or psychic capacity.

But what is a house if not a big object?

In residual haunting cases, people report seeing (or hearing or feeling or smelling) a presence (or several) typically engaged in some sort of activity. It could be a man's figure walking up and down the hallway, or footsteps heard from the attic, or a man and woman physically fighting until one is dead, or even the sounds of two people making love coming from an adjoining room.

The events and figures witnessed in such cases tend to be repetitive both in what's experienced and when they occur (at approximately the same time). Speaking with the figures tends to do no good, because they just continue to go about their business, as though you're not even there. In other words, they're essentially holograms instead of conscious beings capable of interacting.

Residual hauntings seem to be some kind of environmental recording of events and people. The house or building or land somehow records its history, with the more emotion-laden events and experiences coming through louder and stronger. That people mostly report negative events and emotions (around suicide, murder, or other violent crimes, or emotional fights) is likely due to a reporting artifact rather than any unbalanced ratio of negative to positive events—people experiencing something negative are more likely to report it or ask for help.

You might think of a residual haunting as a loop of video or audio tape playing itself over and over for you to watch. Trying to interact with the impression would be akin to trying to interact with a show on your television—you can turn it off or change the channel, but you wouldn't expect the actors to suddenly stop and talk to you directly.

What about the role of technology in investigations? Don't you need technology to make the investigation scientific?

First of all, using technological devices does not make an investigation scientific. It's the application of scientific—physical and social sciences—methodologies that applies here. Unless a sensing device is used properly (and too many amateurs haven't even read or understood the instructions) *and* the data gathered is appropriately assessed and applied, there's nothing scientific about its use.

As we discuss the cases throughout the book, Loyd will explain the type of equipment used, why it was first used, and how useful it is in the investigations.

Secondly, we *define* these phenomena based on human experience and observation. A ghost *is* consciousness. A residual haunting is a *result* of interactions with human consciousness. A poltergeist is *caused* by human consciousness though, at least in these cases, the physical effects can be observed by all and recorded, since they are physical.

So, unless the data gathered from the tech devices is correlated with human experiences of something unusual or paranormal, such as those of a psychic, you simply have anomalous—or unexplained—"readings." *Not* necessarily anything paranormal.

The Queen Anne Hotel

1590 Sutter Street
San Francisco

This unique Victorian building began its life in 1890 as a boarding school, known as the Miss Mary Lake's School for Girls. Over the next few decades it transformed into the Cosmos Gentleman's Club, before becoming the Episcopal Dioceses' Girls Friendly Society Lodge. The building endured a period of fifty years of disuse until 1980, when it was carefully renovated and finally reopened in 1995 as the 48-room Queen Anne hotel. We visited the hotel in September 2009. What follows is a combination narrative and transcript of our visit.

LOYD: I had been to the Queen Anne Hotel a couple of times before. The first time was a few years ago when I was invited to go on the then-fledgling San Francisco Ghost Hunt tour (sfghosthunt.com), run by my good friend Jim Fassbinder—himself a member of the Office of Paranormal Investigations group. Since then, Jim had told me that he ran into many people staying in the hotel who had had encounters with the ghost, and our most recent visit supported that the place was definitely still active.

One of the most important factors in deciding to investigate a haunted location is whether the place has current—or at least recent—reported activity. The reason for this is that sometimes the case can be "cold." In the case of residual haunting, the events impressed into the environment may have been essentially recorded over by enough subsequent activity that the haunting is essentially now like background static. For apparition cases, ghosts can move on to the Light or even decide to head out to other locations. Because they have free will, they're only stuck if they believe they are.

Investigating a location without current phenomena can still be interesting from an information-gathering perspective, but bringing in a world-class psychic/medium like Annette to such a location is almost a waste of her time.

Both Jim Fassbinder and the manager of the hotel, Michael Wade, assured me that they'd heard recent reports of encounters with apparitions at the Queen Anne.

I knew Annette had not been there, and thought it would be a great place to take her, especially given how many people still visit through Jim Fassbinder's nightly tour and the numerous guests who stay at the Hotel.

ANNETTE: Loyd and I walked into the charming Victorian Queen Anne Hotel on the corner of Sutter and Octavia in Pacific Heights. We were accompanied by Dr. Michael Sudduth, a philosophy professor and colleague of Loyd's who had volunteered to be our videographer for the day. We were greeted warmly by the manager.

The hotel lobby was beautifully decorated with Victorian heirloom antiques and had a nice cozy, warm feeling about it. There were many

The hotel lobby

overstuffed chairs and love seats in the large main lobby, with clusters of small wooden tables in between. A magnificent dark mahogany original sideboard with a top to match, filled with silver cups and photos, flanked the southern wall. An walnut 1890 Steinway grand piano filled the room on the west side, draped with an ornate brocaded antique cloth with fringe. A wooden staircase on the east side of the room, with nicely polished walnut handrails, led up to the adjoining three floors. At the far end of this room was another smaller room with a marble-faced fireplace across from the open white-framed French doors.

I joined the boys and we sat down in the southern end of the large twenty-foot-by-twenty-foot lobby and spoke with the manager. After a brief conversation, we began our investigation of the supposed ghost originating from the time of the Mary Lake's School for Girls, which had occupied the building from February 15, 1890 through 1896.

I wanted to start back down in the smaller ante room where the ladies room adjoined the lobby. Loyd agreed and off we went with Michael, camera in hand, ready for anything that might occur. As I walked back into

The room off the lobby

that room, I immediately began to see a wooden desk form in front of the large western window.

LOYD: Working with Annette over the years, I've learned to spot subtle signs that she's about to "get" information. There's something about her demeanor that changes when psychically perceiving the past—those residual impressions—as opposed to normal perception or even the perception of apparitions. As we walked into the ante room, it was pretty clear that there was something impressed into the environment.

ANNETTE: *I keep getting a big desk here, and a woman with her back to the window.* [Annette moving her hands around in a circle] *This is an impression. I feel that this was Mary Lake's office. The children would come in here to talk with her. There are books over there in the eastern corner where a bookcase once stood.*

[Turning to Loyd] *Oh, Mary Lake, the mistress, I feel that she had this childlike quality.*

Loyd, when I went into the ladies room, earlier, that door on the right. I was looking in the mirror, checking my makeup and hair. I heard a female voice say, "Make sure that you wash your hands!" I responded out loud with, "Oh, hello

Mary!' I had been talking to her in my mind a few minutes before, to see if she would know that I was there and talk to me. Well, I certainly did wash my hands and had a really good feeling.

LOYD: I turned on the electromagnetic field (EMF) meter I had. I'd been taking general readings since we came into the hotel, with the majority at the expected .5 to 1.5 milligauss—what most homes and buildings register. I told Annette and Michael that we were suddenly registering 2.5 milligauss in the room where Mary Lake had her office. Not a significant difference, but a difference with no apparent natural/technological cause.

ANNETTE: *Loyd, I am not surprised that this was her office. There were chairs around the desk where the students would sit when she talked to them or anyone else who came in here.*

LOYD: After a few moments of looking around and no other impressions showing up, Michael and I followed Annette back to the main lobby, and to the center of the room. Several guests had come in and were milling around, but Annette just ignored them. However, it was clear to me that she was not ignoring something else, and she began speaking with a ghost she was perceiving.

ANNETTE: *It's very cold right here. I am picking something up, there is a young girl. She has long blond hair, kind of giggling.*

She is dancing around in circles and I am covered with goosebumps! This is not an impression but a definite ghost! [Pause] *I asked her who she was. She said that she "loved Miss Mary." She called her Miss Mary.*

LOYD: We observed Annette turning her head, as if she is listening. Her side of the conversation with the ghost—and relating it to us—was punctuated by pauses and a bit of laughter now and then.

ANNETTE: *She has a bit of a southern accent, and she would just go bouncing into Miss Mary's office and Miss Mary would always smile when she came in, as she was so full of energy.*

LOYD: *Do you have a name for her?*

ANNETTE: *Yes, she says her name is Lilly.* [Annette laughs a little] *And she loves flowers and in the back she would pick flowers.* [Annette opens her eyes and turns to Loyd] *They must have had some kind of garden in the back. She's telling me that she likes to stay here in this room because she likes the people. Lilly dances in this room but they can't see her. She likes to do ballet and so would dance around. She is so happy to have an audience, but she knows they cannot see her. Lilly is so cute; she looks to be between eight and eleven years old.*

LOYD: Annette would occasionally speak directly to the ghost, pretty much for our benefit, since the communication was actually telepathic.

Artist's conception of the ghost of Lilly

ANNETTE: *Where do you come from Lilly?* [Annette pauses to listen] *Her mother died and her father sent her here. She is from Texas. She says, "At first the girls didn't like me because of the way I talked. But they finally stopped making fun of me."*

LOYD: When we moved back into the lobby, the EMF meter's reading fell to a more normal 1.5 milligauss. I began moving a bit to see if I could get any difference in and around where Annette was directing her attention. In apparition cases, the field tends to be mobile, as if the ghost is interacting with the magnetic environment. It also often has bigger changes when Annette perceives an emotional reaction to specific questions on the part of the ghost.

ANNETTE: *Why do you stay here, Lilly? Why haven't you gone into the Light?*

LOYD: We had a jump on the meter at that moment. It was 1.5 and topped out with the setting's range (up to 3 milligauss on one setting; up to 100 milligauss on another setting).

ANNETTE: *Lilly is telling me that she didn't go into the Light because of being afraid. She likes it here because of all the people that come and she can play and can have company. She wants to stay here and doesn't want to leave.* [Annette turns to Loyd] *I don't think we want to send her into the Light.*

LOYD: *No, we don't want to force her. Does she know that she can go?*

The EMF meters were fluctuating up and down with no apparent cause, showing that there was something quite energetic going on.

ANNETTE: [Talking directly to the ghost] *Do you know that you can go into the light, Lilly?* [A pause, Annette turns to Loyd and repeats what Lilly said to her] *"Yes, but I don't want to go."*

ANNETTE: [Talking directly to the ghost] *Alright Lilly.* [Annette laughing and then exclaiming] *Oh, she wants to hold my hand!*

LOYD: *Ok, have her hold your hand as we go upstairs.*

ANNETTE: We headed for the elevators, and inside the small elevator was a bench along the left hand side. I felt strongly that I had to sit down with Lilly on the bench as we rode up to the fourth floor. Loyd and Michael were standing with their backs facing the door of the elevator.

As soon as the door closed we all felt this sudden surge of energy and I saw Loyd reel back a bit.

LOYD: I felt a strong wave of something pass through me, something I've felt in other haunted locations over the years. I could see Annette react, but I wasn't sure if she'd felt it or if she was reacting to my experience.

LOYD: *Whoah! Annette did you feel that?*

ANNETTE: *Absolutely!*

Landing on the fourth floor we began walking down the hall to room 410, where Mary Lake had her apartment. We couldn't get into the room as it was occupied by hotel guests, so we stood in the hallway, outside her door. Immediately I began to pick up on Mary Lake.

ANNETTE: *Mary thinks, Loyd, that you are very nice.* [Annette smiles broadly]

LOYD: [Excited] *Oh, did she come in the elevator with us?*

ANNETTE: [Giggling a bit] *Yes!* [Annette's eyes close] *Yes, and she is very happy and excited to see you.*

[Annette puts her hand to her heart] *Oh, my heart is just palpitating.* [Annette took another deep breath and went on.] *Mary, is happy as she does want the world to know that she is here. She is telling me that she did not die here, but that she came back to her home because this was the happiest time of her life.*

[Annette pauses a moment] *And, ah, she was loved. She couldn't have her own children so these young girls became her children.*

[A lengthy pause and Annette's eyes open] *She is saying, "I am delighted to meet you. I have been waiting for someone to come to talk to me. So that I can tell you how happy my life was while I was living here and teaching the children, and how I helped these young girls become ladies."*

Outside the most haunted room

"It was very important to me that they become ladies and understand about manners of what to do and not to do. And the etiquette that they learned here and the studies were so very important. It was like I was creating a finishing school for these young women, to be able to go out into society."

LOYD: Mary Lake seemed to be coming through Annette quite strongly, and she continued in rapid-fire monologue, as though she (Mary) thought her time in conversation could be cut off at any moment.

ANNETTE: *"Many of these girls were from very wealthy families that were trusted in my care."*

[A long pause, then Annette closes her eyes again] *"I walk through and sometimes I dress up and wear a very fancy hat and sometimes I wear a long pretty gown and walk down the stairs. Sometimes people have seen me and are quite surprised. Then I have to kind of make myself disappear, because I don't want to frighten them. I just want them to understand that our being, our thoughts are always here. And my thoughts are always here and my thoughts are still of these lovely young women and I so yearn to see them again. Lilly is here with me and keeps me company. This is wonderful, but I want to see the rest of my children, but they don't come."*

Artist's conception of Mary Lake with Annette and Loyd

LOYD: [Addressing Mary directly] *Maybe they have moved on?*
ANNETTE: *Yes,* [Sigh] *yes.*
LOYD: [Talking to Annette] *Has she thought of moving on as well?*
ANNETTE: [Annette talking directly to the ghost] *Mary, have you given any thought to moving into the light and going to the other side?*

[Pause, Annette's eyes tightly close at this point] *No, no she does not want to do that.* [Sigh] *She is telling me about her family. Her family ... she doesn't know her family. She says, she was an orphan and doesn't know who they are and so she prefers to stay here with Lilly and with the energies of the children.*

LOYD: [Leaning closer to Annette] *With the energy that is here? Is she afraid of what's out there?*
ANNETTE: [Pause and then a sigh] *She says she has great trepidation.*
LOYD: [Nodding in agreement] *Ok!*
ANNETTE: *Mary say, "Yes, and my sweetpie, he is with his family. He is with his family, so I can't go there."*

LOYD: Annette seemed to get quite emotional and, as though Mary was acting through her, seemed to hold back tears as Mary mentioned a man she loved in life. Also interesting was the term "sweetpie" as opposed to the usual "sweetie-pie."

ANNETTE: Her sweetpie was Senator James Graham Fair, who had become extremely wealthy during the Gold Rush from the Comstock Lode in Nevada. He had built the building and totally financed the school and soon became involved with Mary Lake after he enrolled his two daughters to keep them close. He and his wife had divorced and this was a way to have his children nearby. He went on to build the first Fairmont Hotel in San Francisco. His two daughters, Theresa and Virginia, did indeed become socialites and married into very wealthy families.

After the death of Senator Fair in 1896, the school lost its financial backing and was closed.

LOYD: *It's a pretty big place there. She probably wouldn't find him, but she could look for her girls. I am not saying that she should leave, just curious to see if she has thought about this.*

ANNETTE: *Mary is saying that she has, but, as she was dying, the decision was not to leave. She wanted to stay.*

LOYD: *She is very comfortable here?*

ANNETTE: *Yes. And she will stay here. She is telling me that she does not want to go.*

LOYD: *How does she feel about the tours every night?*

ANNETTE: *Mary thinks they're wonderful. She comes downstairs to see them.* [Pause] *She looks out the window a lot, but isn't sure if anyone has ever seen her in the window.* [Annette again relays Mary's words] *"It makes me feel good that they understand that I am here. I don't want them to be afraid, but be aware and understand that this is possible. That a human being can do this."*

[Annette turns to Loyd] *Ok, what I am feeling from Mary is this philosophy, that she seems to understand this philosophy without having any formal background.*

LOYD: [Smiling] *She understands who she is and what she is?*

ANNETTE: *Yes, she understands that she is in this consciousness and that she is a ghost.* [Annette nods her head in further confirmation] *She understands that very well and she is very happy here.*

LOYD: *Does she know how she is communicating with people or being seen? The process?*

ANNETTE: [After a long pause] *Mary knows when they see her. She is telling me she goes down the hallway and goes down the stairs a great deal. The cleaning people will catch a glimpse of her at times. She is aware that they can see her.* [Pause] *She has a way of sort of backing off and disappearing.*

LOYD: *Backing off?*

ANNETTE: *Yes, she backs off.* [Pause; Annette's eyes tightly shut and she speaks to the ghost] *How do you do that Mary? How do you make yourself disappear?* [Long pause]

She knows how to increase her energy and how to decrease her energy. So when she thinks they have seen her, she pulls back her energy and they can't see her anymore.

[Pause] *Yes, that's what it is. When it's safe and ok, she will be very visible. If someone happened to get off the elevator or came up the stairs and she was standing here, Mary would pull back and become invisible.*

[Speaking as Mary] *"I know that many people have seen me. I want to say hello but don't want to frighten anybody. But some people have been sort of in a state of shock and so then I will pull back immediately."*

LOYD: *So that was her that we felt in the elevator?*

ANNETTE: [Nodding] *Yes, yes, that was her in the elevator.* [Laughing] *And she wanted to know who these people were that Lilly was coming with.* [More laughter from Annette] *She and Lilly are wonderful friends and keep each other company.*

LOYD: *Should we walk around here a little bit?*

ANNETTE: *Yes, ok.* [Annette takes in a deep breath and rubs her eyes]

LOYD: As we continued through the hotel, things got a bit philosophical. After all, Michael Sudduth *is* a professor of philosophy. The question of what the Afterlife is like came up, whether Mary knew if there was a Heaven or Hell, and so on.

In my years investigating apparition cases where there was communication with the deceased consciousness present, as well as looking into the question from the literature containing such conversations, it seemed to me that those we call ghosts or apparitions—what Annette and others refer to as "earthbound" entities because they have not moved on to the Light or other side—are often ignorant of what's next or afraid of what's there.

Michael jumped in with some directed questions about this, about her existence as an apparition, especially how much of our interaction with her could be from us, rather than from her—tough in some respects, these were not necessarily questions we expected to have Mary address.

MICHAEL: *Is this something that we project? Our experience of what an apparition is? Could it be that she is not experiencing this? It's not her own beliefs and desires, her experience in the afterlife, but our projections instead? So for her these are not realties?*

LOYD: We also put out the question of her expectation of how the next step would be for her. I wondered whether her expectations could make the existence she wanted a reality.

MICHAEL: *I think so, I think there is a possibility of existence and what it's like being shaped in the afterlife. Maybe she can tell me something about that.*

ANNETTE: [As Mary] *"It is difficult to imagine Hell, because I have not experienced that, even though I am not in a physical body I am free to think, free to move. I do not sleep or eat."*

LOYD: *Does she know about time? How time passes?*

ANNETTE: [Pause] *"It just flows, it moves. I am not aware of days or years or time—it just moves. I know the difference in time by the way they dress, by the way they behave."*

[Annette turns to Loyd] *That is how she has been able to understand that there is passage of time.*

LOYD: [Nodding as if in agreement] *Ok, observational. She observes.*

ANNETTE: *She is observing things around here. When she was in a physical form, time was of the essence and the clock was her god, because everything had to be on time to teach her girls.* [Annette laughs loudly] *But now it's wonderful because she doesn't have to worry about time!*

MICHAEL: *Is she happy?*

ANNETTE: [Smiling] *She is telling me how ecstatic she is.*

[As Mary] *"I know that everyone would not choose to do what I am doing. But I am very happy in this state, so happy being here. This was the home and love of my life."*

MICHAEL: [Leaning forward] *So she knows something of the joy of Heaven?*

ANNETTE: [As Mary, smiling] *"Oh, yes … I understand and that would be the joy, the happiness that I am experiencing. There is no pain, no sadness. I have really no sadness, per se. I don't feel lonely, I am content."*

MICHAEL: [Turning and speaking directly to Loyd] *This may be her heaven.*

ANNETTE: *Mary says, "I agree, and this is what I wanted to ask you."*

MICHAEL: [Turning to Loyd again] *How did she know that I was involved with philosophy?*

LOYD: *She may have picked this out of your head, Annette. You may not have remembered but I had mentioned it to you.*

ANNETTE: [Eyes closed tightly again] *How did you know that Mary?* [Annette stammers a bit, as if startled] *Yes, yes, she can read my mind. Alright!*

Heading down from the fourth floor

Mary, is saying something to me: "One of the things that I liked to teach the girls was about French history and how you need to curtsy and be a good listener."

Loyd said he got the feeling that we had spoken to Mary enough there on the fourth floor, and suggested we go downstairs to another location we needed to check. We began walking down the stairs.

As we approached the second floor, a woman who was a guest watched us for a moment. As if deciding we were people she could speak to, she approached and told us that she saw something down the hallway last night. She thought it was a woman and just wanted us to know.

LOYD: I surmised that seeing us with a camcorder and EMF meters probably was a dead giveaway that we were there to check out the reported haunting. This is something that happens to us often when visiting public places with reported phenomena, and is a benefit to being in those places when there are people present (as opposed to the now-stereotyped after-hours stakeouts).

ANNETTE: We entered one of the bedrooms, 210, which the manager had mentioned had also had reported activity; the room also contained a

On the 2nd floor

plant that a guest requested be placed there, after encountering and having a conversation with Mary. I looked around to see what was there. Mary had apparently followed us.

ANNETTE: *Ok, Loyd. Mary, is telling me that she did come in here because this gentleman was really sad and he was alone and he needed some tender loving. She tucked him in once when he was asleep. Lilly came in with her and stayed with him. Mary was concerned about his heart.*

LOYD: *Annette, here is the plant that the guest told the manager to get based on what Mary had reportedly told one of the guests.*

ANNETTE: [Looking puzzled] *Ok, Mary, what about the woman that you told to have a plant in the room?* [Annette pauses to listen to Mary's response] *This woman would hold her breath while she was sleeping, she didn't have enough oxygen. This is why Mary told her intuitively that she needed a plant in the room to supply more oxygen. After she went back home from her trip she ordered a plant and had it delivered to the hotel for this specific room.*

Mary is saying, "When the girls were upstairs, she always made sure that they had the windows open so they would have enough oxygen."

[Annette asks the ghost a direct question aloud] *Mary, do you go and check on the people to make sure that they are alright during the night? I have a feeling that you may do that sometimes.*

[Annette listens and laughs loudly] *She says, "You caught me. I do. I want to make sure that everyone is comfortable, that they rest well. That they are being completely taken care of and they are enjoying every moment. That is very important to me that everyone is having this wonderful, happy experience."*

LOYD: It's always interesting to watch Annette switch back and forth between quoting the ghosts, summarizing what they're saying, and this kind of back and forth dialogue.

ANNETTE: *Very wonderful, Mary, thank you for doing that, it is terribly important. And perhaps this is why many of the people come back to this lovely hotel, because they have a very wonderful experience here in this building.*

LOYD: Apparently Lilly had also accompanied us to room 210.

ANNETTE: [After a long pause and a big laugh] *Lilly says, "There are not enough flowers. They need real flowers in the hotel and in the rooms, because flowers make people happy."*

MICHAEL: *Is Mary aware of any other spirits in the hotel?*

ANNETTE: *No, she says there is only herself and Lilly. And Lilly dances for her every night and she just loves that. They are wonderful friends.*

Lilly wanted to be a ballerina and is very sad at times because she didn't get to do that. Mary says, "She hurt her leg. She fell, from the ankle to the knee there was a fracture, the bones broke. This kept her from becoming a dancer. This led to a long recuperation, and Lilly then contracted pneumonia and sadly it took her life."

[Continuing as Mary] *"I was with her when she passed. Lilly said she didn't want to leave me. And I said to her, she didn't have to. And so this is why Lilly is here with me. So Lilly was here first and when I passed I came back to be here with Lilly and to be in the place that I loved, my home."*

"It was so difficult leaving when I had to close the school. I always knew in my heart that I would come back. In one way or another I would come back and I knew that Lilly would be here waiting for me—and she was."

[Annette, seemingly overcome with emotion, talks directly to the ghost] *Thank you Mary, that was very nice.*

LOYD: [Trying to lighten up the conversation] *Annette, have Lilly and Mary looked around San Francisco these days? Or do they just pretty much stay here in the building?*

ANNETTE: [As Mary] *"We just stay here."*

LOYD: *Does she know that she can go and come back?*

ANNETTE: *"Umm ... Yes, but I am apprehensive about leaving the building."*

LOYD: [Speaking directly to Mary] *But Mary, it's ok, you can come back again. You and Lilly can go and take a walk outside and look around; it's alright, and you will be able to come back. So that is definitely an option for you. You might want to consider that at some other time.*

We know this from other ghosts who can travel far and then come back to their own place. They get to see great places around the world, for free.

[Loyd smiles at Annette and Michael] *Here I am again being a ghost travel agent.*

ANNETTE: *She is shaking her head. Yes, she will think about it.* [Laughing and turning to Loyd] *She's not sure.*

LOYD: *I want to make her afterlife as fun as possible. If she gets bored, she could take Lilly with her and they could go to the zoo.*

ANNETTE: [Laughing and very animated like a child] *Oh, Lilly is jumping up and down.*

LOYD: *They could go see the King Tut exhibit at the De Young Museum. They could go to plays, and all for free.*

ANNETTE: [Still animated and laughing] *Lilly is saying, "Yes, yes, let's do that, let's do that!"*

[A pause] *Mary is asking me, "Is that really possible?"*

[Annette nods her head in affirmation of the point, then speaks directly to the ghost] *Yes, Mary, it is possible. You will come back! You can will yourself there as well. You just have to think about it. I know that you know how to do this, as you will yourself in this building. So you might want to experiment with that.*

Mary says that she "will think about it."

LOYD: *She could even practice by taking the ghost tour; and I believe they start and end here, as well. So she could go out and come back with them and listen to the other ghost stories of places around here.*

ANNETTE: [Again talking directly to the ghost] *And also Mary, maybe meeting some other ghosts.* [Annette starts laughing very hard] *Oh dear, that's a lot. She is a little overwhelmed.*

LOYD: [Laughs as well] *We should probably go downstairs and let her think about it.*

ANNETTE: [Rubbing the top of her head] *Oh, the top of my head hurts.*

After I have channeled ghosts for a long period of time, my frontal lobe will begin to throb a bit, and indeed it *was* throbbing.

We walked down the hall, at the end of which was a very large ornate wooden-encased floor-to-ceiling mirror.

MICHAEL: *Annette, is there anything in this mirror?*

A special mirror

ANNETTE: [after a long pause] *Yes, she has looked in this mirror, especially when she wears her lovely hat. She will come down the stairs to see herself in the mirror, with her hat on. She is saying that she wants to make sure that she looks cultured in her hat.*

LOYD: Even after giving Mary so much to consider, apparently she stuck with us.

ANNETTE: *Mary, you always look cultured. I see you wearing the hat and you look gorgeous.* [Turning towards Michael] *Mary thinks some people have seen her in the mirror.*

LOYD: Indeed, this was confirmed by reports.

ANNETTE: *Mary is telling me that this mirror is an original piece that belonged to the house. And when the girls were dancing they would run downstairs to look at themselves first in the mirror to make sure that they looked nice and were altogether and beautiful. It was a very special place where the girls loved to come.*

And other times when she is wearing a long dress she will come and admire herself in the mirror—she gets flashbacks of the girls being here, around her, and remembering the laughter, the joy. She does a lot of reminiscing about those wonderful times that were here.

[After a short pause] *She is asking me, "Isn't it beautiful?"*

Yes, Mary, the mirror is beautiful and so are you! I am so glad, Mary, that you enjoy it, and that you look at yourself.

I think it's wonderful, and that tells me a lot about what it feels like being in the form that you are in. And that you are still concerned about yourself. That tells me and verifies that our consciousness does stay the same. As we were in life, we are in death. And so this is a wonderful validation. Thank you.

LOYD: It seemed at that moment that Mary was leaving us on our own. So, we headed back downstairs and gathered our equipment together and said our good-byes to the manager and to the Queen Anne Hotel, for the moment at least.

We headed out to meet Jim Fassbinder for lunch, eager to let him know of our experiences in the Queen Anne with Mary and Lilly so he could add to his already rich-with-information ghost tour of the Pacific Heights neighborhood.

A Few Words from the Parapsychologist

It's always fascinating to visit a location like the Queen Anne Hotel, which has more than one friendly ghost in residence, and to run into folks on the fly who offer us their own interesting stories and encounters. Over the years, this has been my own experience when it's known who and what I am, and I know Annette encounters the same.

From a hard science perspective, the experiences of the witnesses and Annette—or my own perceptions for that matter—are not worth much. They are purely subjective evidence that something is happening, though the disbelievers out there will comment that it's "suggestion" or "expectation" or something similar.

But it's those very experiences which define the paranormal or psychic. In fact, all human experience is subjective, but it is that experience which defines the way we see our world and try to further explain it.

The Queen Anne Hotel is a rich location for those interested in the paranormal to have potential encounters with at least two people who are in a different state of existence. They no longer have bodies, but they are still able to interact with us on some level, though of course some of us get more of an interaction than others.

Annette's perceptions and communications with Mary and Lilly are right in keeping with the experiences reported by many others, and seem to fit the history of the building in its previous incarnation. That the hotel staff, as well as ghost tour impresario Jim Fassbinder, had heard about and continue to hear of experiences with Mary and Lilly relayed by their guests and customers supports the existence of that paranormal "something" we call ghosts.

It is the growing number of experiences of regular people, plus the insights of the more perceptive such as Annette Martin, that builds up the evidence for the existence of ghosts. The technology used in investigations, in this case simple EMF detectors, when coupled with many people's reports of their own encounters, further supports the observation that something created by non-normal causes is occurring.

But it is the *experiences* which shout "Ghost!" Not a simple rise in magnetic fields.

For those of you planning on visiting the Queen Anne Hotel in hopes of meeting Lilly and Mary, consider this old adage: "You catch more flies with honey …."

Stay at the hotel with an open and friendly mind and demeanor. Ask nicely for a visitation from Mary and Lilly, and if you see them, say hello to them from Annette and Loyd. But if they're not around, don't despair.

Mary might have taken Lilly to the Zoo!

The Mansions Hotel

2220 Sacramento Street
San Francisco

(Note: This is no longer a hotel open to the public. It is now a private residence. Please be respectful of the residents).

The Mansions Hotel (drawing courtesy Pat Hunter)

LOYD: This case is a unique situation for the scope of this book. The Mansions Hotel was sold off several years ago and is no longer a hotel, having been converted to private residences. That in itself makes it different from the rest of the locations in this book, which are public. One can still find listings and reviews for the place as a hotel on the web thanks to the amount of old info in cyberspace that never goes away.

Even though it may not be a place to walk into, or even haunted for that matter, it is known as a San Francisco haunted landmark. Annette and I both felt that our own observations of the place would still be of interest to our readers. Though you can't visit the building on the inside unless you know someone who lives there, you can certainly swing by the location when you visit the Queen Anne Hotel, which is relatively close. Both buildings are in the Pacific Heights area of San Francisco.

One other interesting tidbit: Annette and I have both been to the Mansions Hotel when it was fully operational as a hotel on different occasions, but never together. So in this case, you really have separate perceptions of what was (and may still be) there.

The Mansions Hotel was composed of two connected Victorian mansions, though, until the late twentieth century, the hotel was just one of the buildings—the one that is most important to our story, since it was the one with the ghost. Built in 1887, the original owner was silver mining magnate Richard Chambers.

Married, with no children, Chambers and his wife lived there for a relatively short time. Chambers died in 1901 sometime after his wife passed away. With no direct heirs, the mansion was willed to two nieces, Claudia Chambers and her sister, of whom little is known. They ended up building a companion home right next to the first, occupied by Claudia's sister. It's not known whether the sisters got along well or not.

Claudia apparently had a freak accident "with blades" that killed her. How she was killed here is a matter of dispute, though the stories range from her being accidentally sawed in half to being killed with knives or some kind of farm tool. Claudia must have loved the home willed to her by her uncle, as apparently even in death she did not want to leave.

In 1977, entertainer Bob Pritikin purchased the property and turned it into The Mansions Hotel and Restaurant. After opening the hotel, Pritikin, his employees, and especially his guests, were surprised to learn that the older of the two buildings was haunted. Accounts from various psychics over the years seem to indicate more than one female ghost walked the halls, popped into rooms, and "played" with the guests. Many accounts, though, support there only being one ghost present: Claudia.

Witnesses reported numerous sightings of a female apparition waking them from their sleep in their hotel rooms, sometimes accompanied by their covers mysteriously being pulled off their beds. During the years that the place was open, guests and employees reported exploding wine glasses, flying objects, inexplicable noises, cold spots, and so on. On rare occasions, witnesses reported a male apparition dressed in Victorian-era clothing.

Pritikin was both a magician and a musician—he played the musical saw (possibly contributing to the idea that Claudia was sawed in half). He had a nightly show following dining in the restaurant that included both of his performing skills, a ghost story (about Claudia), and several illusions and special effects that played off the ghostly presence. It's been suggested that the activity might have been a result of Claudia's displeasure of the state of her home, as well her critique of Pritikin's show. But no one was ever harmed by the ghost (or ghosts).

While it was open, I visited the Mansions Hotel several times, attended a couple of Pritikin's shows, and investigated the place a bit. But before I tell you about my own visits, let me turn it over to Annette to tell you her experience there.

ANNETTE: In the fall of 1997, I was contacted by the History Channel and asked to participate in a special TV presentation of *Haunted History of San Francisco*.

Needless to say I was thrilled, as San Francisco is my home town. The special would be about the history of the city, its place in America's past, and, of course, the spirits that may still walk the streets and inhabit the dwellings.

I asked where they were going to be filming and was told that the Winchester Mystery House in San Jose was one location, and that the other spot was going to be a secret destination.

Well, that was intriguing for me and I immediately responded with, "Oh, how exciting, a new place for me to investigate and explore!" The producer laughed and was delighted that I would see this as an adventure.

Three weeks later, I was on my way to San Francisco with a map of where I was to meet the film crew. Upon arriving at 2220 Sacramento Street and finding a place to park I embarked up the steep stairs to this palatial, elegant residence. There were no obvious signs saying whether or not this was a private residence or a B &B or hotel.

I knocked on the door and a short young man, smiling from ear to ear opened the door and greeted me by name. Obviously they were expecting me, I thought to myself.

I was ushered into a foyer that was like stepping back into the 1800s. Magnificently decorated and quite eclectic, it had an air of something very different. I could hear classical music—I believed that it was Bach—as I was trying to sort out what was embedded in this mansion. A slim, soft spoken woman of Spanish descent approached and asked me to follow her. We walked down a long hallway with rich walnut wood paneling on the walls and turned to the left to be greeted by another young woman who introduced herself as the director of the show segment. We were then ushered into a small dining room where we enjoyed a cup of coffee with the crew—and then it was off to explore this incredible house.

The director asked me if I had ever been here before. "No, I haven't," I replied.

She nodded her head and smiled. "Good!"

The camera crew went ahead as we began walking through a sitting room decorated with sofas covered in red crushed velvet and lavishly brocaded wall hangings and chairs to match. Interesting antiques were everywhere (my parents were in the antique business for years, so I happen to have an eye for them). There was a magnificent fireplace, with little ceramic and wooden pigs sitting on the mantel and on side tables. The pigs definitely looked out of place with all the ornate designs and antiques, but who am I to criticize? [Note from Loyd: You'll learn about the significance of the pigs when you get to my story.] Magnificent crystal chandeliers abound throughout the rooms and hallways.

We continued on and came to a lovely wooden staircase. I began to get little goose bumps here and there on my arms and said, "Oh, there is some energy here!"

She said, "Good, let's start by you walking up the staircase. Action!" she told the crew.

I climbed several stairs and broke out in goose bumps—looking up, I saw standing at the top of the stairs a very distinguished man dressed in an elegant Victorian style black suit. He was quite tall, and his brown hair and grey dusted sideburns added to his air of sophistication. He was just staring at me. I said out loud, "Hello, my name is Annette Martin." There was a bit of a smile on his face, but he didn't offer a reply. I asked another question: "Is this your house?" He nodded his head "yes." I moved to climb the next stair to get a better look and he began to fade away until there was nothing there.

"This gentleman is definitely a ghost," I announced, "and I have a feeling that he might have built the house as well as being the owner."

The director called out and asked me to continue to the top of the stairs.

When I reached the top, there was a magnificent hardwood floor landing about seven feet long, so I continued walking with the cameras constantly going.

There was a little turn at the end of the landing going into another hallway, but just as I turned I saw a large picture of a man hanging on the wall. I walked up to get a better look and exclaimed, "This is the man that I just saw! Is this the man who built and owned this house?"

The director answered from behind the camera, "We believe that he is. This is Richard Chambers who built the house for himself."

They directed me down the hallway and we made a left hand turn to discover many doorways with numbers above each one. I began to realize that this home had been turned into a hotel or a bed and breakfast.

The director said, "Pick a door and go into the room, any door."

I was a little annoyed by this as I felt she was definitely testing my abilities. Dismissing my emotions I closed my eyes, took a couple of deep breaths and tried to focus on the hallway to see which door was the one that I was suppose to go into.

I walked up and down with my hands outstretched, using my hands like a dowsing rod, to see where the energy would pull me and finally I felt a coldness that I knew had to do with a particular room. I pointed to the door and went to open it. It opened with little effort. I immediately felt death in the room in the bitterly cold room. The feeling was overwhelming. I walked in cautiously, not knowing what I would find in there.

"Oh," I said out loud. "It is so cold in here and I feel a great deal of loneliness and, and," I stumbled, "sadness." Taking another deep breath and walking further into the room, I said, "Someone was murdered in this room! I hear screaming and feel someone being chased. It feels female and I think another female is chasing her and trying to stab her. They feel related somehow, not sure if they are sisters or cousins. The one female does get murdered but the body is being taken out of this room! The energy in here is so sad!"

On the left of the room was another door, and I wanted to open it and investigate. Upon opening the door, I saw a flash of something white and the toilet flushed all by itself—but no one was there.

I turned to the camera and said, "People who have been in this room have had experiences of a female ghost who comes in and is trying to tell them that something terrible had happened in here. She goes and flushes the toilet and will also play with the TV that is over in the corner, to try and get their attention."

The director interrupted and said "There is someone here who would like to tell you something, Annette."

A young, slim man came out from behind the camera. He was shy, but spoke up and said, "I have come in this room to clean many times and while making the bed, the toilet will flush several times and the TV will come on and off. And it is always cold in here, but not in the other bedrooms. The first time I ran out of the room, but I have now become accustom to the ghost and tell her that I will be finished in a few minutes. The other maids will not come in here!"

"Yes, this is a young woman who was murdered in this room and then taken someplace else," I responded.

"Let's move on, Annette," The director called out. The camera men backed out of the room and headed down the hallway again. "We are going to go up to the Presidential Suite on the third floor."

We climbed another set of stairs and I opened the door to a room facing south. "What a lovely room," I exclaimed.

The room had a high ceiling and off-white walls. There was a raised, canopied, queen-size bed with a gold and white brocaded bedspread. Mirrors were all around. A fireplace and a private wrought-iron balcony that overlooked the grounds added to the ambience.

I sat gingerly on the bed, closed my eyes for a moment, and said, "I feel that our woman who had been murdered loved to come to this room and felt very protective of it, because it was her bedroom."

"Yes, that is correct, Annette, this is her bedroom," the director explained from behind the camera.

"If a guest stayed in this room," I said, "and was not a nice person, I saw the female ghost doing things like throwing things around, like maybe a book or throwing a glass down on the floor and trying to get that person out of her bedroom."

The director interrupted again, "Yes, a gentleman and his wife were staying in this room, which was indeed the bedroom of the murdered girl. As they were getting ready for bed, suddenly a book flew off the bookshelf and landed across the room. The couple was so unnerved by this that they immediately went down to the front desk and said that they were leaving, as there was something very strange about their room."

The director went on, "Also, several people have had the covers pulled up, exposing their feet and scaring them half to death in this bed."

I laughed a bit and responded with, "Yes, she doesn't want anyone in here that would have a negative attitude. I feel that she knows that she is dead but still holds this room dear to her heart."

I closed my eyes again for several minutes, to see if I could see or talk to the female ghost, but nothing came.

LOYD: Annette's experience there was typical of so many of my visits to haunted places with her. I have to say I'm sorry I wasn't present at the time, especially since I also worked on segments of that same episode of *Haunted History*, though at other locations.

As for my visits to the Mansions Hotel, my first was in the very early 1990s for a local TV news show. I got there a bit early, and was told to wait in the foyer for the owner and the producer, who were elsewhere in the hotel. I'd done a bit of checking on the hotel, as I usually like to know something about a place before going in, especially if there's a chance it might be subject to exaggerated stories.

One of the things I'd learned from local newspaper clippings was that some of the witnesses were folks visiting the medical center across the street (currently the California Pacific Medical Center). In a stroke of synchronicity, I happened to overhear a conversation happening at the registration desk.

A woman had come in right behind me and stepped up to the desk after the clerk had informed me that Bob Pritikin would be right with me. She wanted to reserve a room for a visiting surgeon, and gave the dates to the clerk. He told her there would be no problem.

"But he doesn't want to stay in the Rose Room," she added.

"Why not?" asked the clerk.

"Well, he says he was a bit freaked out last time he stayed there because the woman's ghost woke him up."

The desk clerk nodded sagely and said, "Not a problem." Business as usual, apparently.

I, on the other hand, perked up and entered the conversation. I told them who I was and why I was there and asked her to elaborate if she could. She informed me that many visiting doctors and lecturers stayed at the Mansions Hotel at least once, but a number of them didn't want to come back, or wanted different rooms than what they had for previous visits.

As for the surgeon she referred to, he'd told her that on his last visit he was sound asleep in his room when he awoke to his covers being pulled off the bed by something unseen. As he sat up to investigate, the form of a woman came into focus, lit up as if the room lights were all on, which they weren't. She smiled at him and disappeared.

Not the scariest of experiences, I commented, but certainly one that could unnerve people easily, especially if the surgeon had not believed in ghosts previously.

The clerk chimed in and said that the surgeon's experience was actually pretty common at the hotel. I asked the woman if she'd be willing to go on camera, and she declined. She finished her business there and left the hotel.

As Bob Pritikin and the news producer came to get me, Kathy Reardon arrived as well. Kathy was one of the psychics I'd been working with for a few years (this was prior to my working with Annette). Kathy—now living on the East Coast—had not been a psychic all her life like Annette. She'd had a psychic opening in the mid 1980s, first working as a channeler and medium, then recognizing her other psychic capacities. Like Annette, she was incredibly down to earth.

Kathy and I spoke with Pritikin for a short while, getting some background about the kinds of experiences people had but not the specific locations in the mansion and nothing about the history of the hotel. As we walked through the main floor to head up to the guest rooms with the camera crew (but not Pritikin), we saw many antiques and lots and lots of pigs. Wood, ceramic, plastic—made from all sorts of materials. We figured we'd have to ask about them, since Kathy didn't perceive anything out of the ordinary.

I pulled out my handy-dandy EMF sensors as we headed up the stairs. For the most part, the readings were quite high all over the building, but really stepped up on the third floor and near other rooms where people had reported unusual activity. In fact, on the third floor, the device was essentially useless as it topped out at its highest reading.

Before you jump to the often-cited, and generally wrong, TV ghost hunter conclusion that the high readings indicated paranormal activity, consider that most EMF meters are frequency-weighted to pick up fields from electricity-based devices, including circuit boxes and even badly shielded electrical wiring in the walls, as well as from high tension power lines.

In this case, we very quickly determined that the readings were a result of wiring in the walls. I can honestly say I've found more bad wiring in places over the years than ghosts or residual hauntings with my EMF meters.

There is evidence that high magnetic fields, even those caused by man-made devices, including wiring, might cause uneasy feelings and even hallucinations. But certainly not anomalous movement of objects.

So, tossing aside my EMF sensors, I let Kathy be the main detector (as I so often do with Annette).

Kathy led us through the hotel, stopping at certain rooms and identifying them as more active than others. She identified the height of activity on the third floor. This, as we later learned, gelled with what had been reported by so many witnesses over the years.

She also had a short conversation with a woman ghost who claimed she'd been killed on the third floor. While Kathy did not get a name to go along with the apparition, the description seemed to match the female figure others had seen who, as we later learned from Bob Pritikin, was most likely Claudia Chambers.

She also got an impression from the ghost that the pigs were important to her in life, but that she had nothing to do with the figurines, statues, and other pig-stuff that decorated the downstairs.

Kathy's perceptions were confirmed by Pritikin, and we heard a bit about Claudia and even Richard Chambers from him. When we asked about the pigs, he said that he had learned that Claudia raised pigs and really loved them when she was alive, so he added the pig figures to the décor in hopes of making her feel more at home. He also made a joke that sometimes a figurine of a pig would be affected by the ghost—so, yes, "sometimes pigs can fly."

I returned to the Mansions Hotel several times after that, attending a couple of the magic-musical saw shows and speaking with other witnesses.

The stories were quite consistent over the years, and the witnesses were often guests rather than employees who, one might suspect, were coached by the owner—though I did not believe so.

The EMF readings on those subsequent visits were still consistently high. How much the ambient EMF might have played in the experiences people had is impossible to say. The consistency of the experiences would suggest that if there was an effect, it was to make the ghost's ability to connect with the witnesses much easier.

As for myself, I did not experience anything on most of my visits. However, there were times I was up on the third floor that I would swear I was being observed by someone, even when no one was with me.

Having read through Annette's experience there, as well as watching the piece on *Haunted History* and talking with Annette about it, it's a real shame I never got the chance to visit the Mansions Hotel with her. While her primary encounter was with Richard Chambers, based on my own research and investigation, I believe Claudia—if that's who else was present—would have opened up to her. Perhaps, the day Annette visited, Claudia was elsewhere, leaving Richard to mind the store, so to speak.

But the Mansions Hotel was most definitely haunted when receiving guests, even though perhaps the guests didn't appreciate having hosts who were ghosts.

Just a side note on the original house: In checking the web while finishing this book, I found a real estate site listing the mansion for sale, accompanied by numerous photos of the interior rooms. Having seen the hotel in its heyday, I have to say that it is more luxurious and welcoming than before. If Claudia, her uncle, or any other ghosts are still there, they're likely to really be happy with the renovation, and to welcome any new occupants.

The Presidio Officers' Club

Anna Marie's Ghost
San Francisco

LOYD: In late 1996, I got a call from a woman who worked in the office at the Presidio Officers' Club in San Francisco. She had seen an article about me in a San Francisco paper and wanted to know if I would be interested in investigating the Officers' Club, which she stated was quite haunted. The catch was that everything would have to be done with total confidentiality. While the Officers' Club was available for rental for events, it was not approved for publicity as a haunted location—at least, not for a few more years, when I made a return visit with TechTV for a piece that was rerun on ABC.

The Presidio is much more than just a collection of a few buildings, as it's quite a large area with a rich history. According to the National Park Service Website:

> The Presidio has a rich cultural history spanning back to the time of the native Ohlone people. The Spanish arrived in 1776 to establish the northernmost outpost of their empire in western North America. The Presidio then fell under Mexican rule for 24 years before the U.S. Army took control of it in 1846. Over 148 years, the U.S. Army transformed the Presidio grounds from mostly empty windswept dunes and scrub to a verdant, preeminent military post. Since 1994, the Presidio has been a part of the Golden Gate National Recreation Area.

I was able to arrange a visit soon after the initial call from the Presidio employee, accompanied by Annette, her husband Bruce Pettyjohn, and videographer David Richardson, who is a member of my Office of Paranormal Investigations research group.

For confidentiality reasons, we'll call the contact at the Officers' Club "Maggie." She'd told me that there were a number of unusual happenings at the now-empty building, though she understood things had occurred there for many, many years. The primary occurrences included a sense of a presence, a female apparition, sounds of footsteps, and other human activity when no one was present. There were occasional unusual unexplained physical phenomena as well.

For me it this was doubly-interesting, as I'd attended a public speaking seminar in the building the year before, in 1995. I can't say I'd had any inkling the place was haunted at that time.

After meeting in the parking lot, the four of us walked into the Officers' Club. But as we passed a big meeting space just inside the building, I felt drawn to an area on a platform near some big windows facing San Francisco Bay. I shook it off and followed Annette, Bruce, and David and met with Maggie in her office.

After I mentioned I'd been there before for a seminar, Annette said she was pretty sure she'd also been there before, in her younger days as a singer and actress.

We wandered about a bit, with Maggie in the lead. I was checking the environmental magnetic fields as Annette was trying to pick up whatever she could. As we walked deeper into the building, we entered the large multi-purpose room where I'd attended the seminar. Annette had an immediate reaction.

ANNETTE: *My gosh, there are rooms everywhere. This is the room that I performed in years ago in the play "Kiss and Tell," by Hugh Herbert. I played Corlis Archer and Barbara Eden played the older sister!*

LOYD: *Really?*

MAGGIE: *They used to have many performances in this room.*

ANNETTE: *Yes, the Barbara Eden of the TV show, "I Dream of Jeanie." I was 15 years old and Barbara and I both were studying with the Elizabeth Holloway School of the Theatre. She had just won the Miss San Francisco title and wanted to become a famous movie star. We toured the Navy, Army, and Marine camps throughout California for three months. She certainly got her wish!*

So, what happened in here?

MAGGIE: [Pointing up to the ceiling] *There was a plastic bottle that was put up there in the rafters. We think it was the ghost.*

LOYD: Maggie then pointed out to us some large plastic water bottles, the multi-gallon type that we think of as water cooler bottles. She told us she'd come into the empty building to work one day, and found one of the water bottles up in the rafters, neatly balanced. The ceiling was at least thirty feet high, and the rafters only a little below that. I grabbed an empty plastic bottle and Annette motioned me to give it to Bruce.

ANNETTE: *Bruce, do you think you can try and throw a plastic bottle up there?*

We thought that Bruce—who's quite tall and played basketball—could perhaps shoot the bottle into the rafters. He tried a couple of times and failed.

BRUCE: *I think with practice it could be done.*

LOYD: *Maggie, you said the bottle was left off the vent. Was it standing up on end?* [She nods "yes"] *Maybe it was lifted up by some other means? Someone could get it up there? Or they were lucky on the second throw?*

Of course, someone with a long ladder could indeed have put the water bottle in the rafters, but Maggie stated that given the circumstances, the limited number of people who had access to the building, and the time available for someone to pull the prank, she said it wasn't possible. To me, that meant very improbable, but not impossible. But what would that someone's motive be?

We moved further into the building....

MAGGIE: *I hate going into the kitchen. It gives me the willies.*

LOYD: We entered the kitchen area, which was apparently still operational for events at which food was called for.

ANNETTE: *There's a cold spot right here.*

LOYD: *Annette, if you get any sensations here, let me know and I will take a picture.*

I was using a Polaroid camera for such pictures. We'd had success with unusual light and what seemed like energetic effects with Polaroid in the past. Polaroid cameras and film were quite different from the norm (and vastly different from digital cameras) in that there was a lengthy chemical process happening with the film from time of exposure.

Parapsychologists view the very concept of photos of ghosts as being film or digital media affected by the mind of the ghost—a psychokinetic (mind over matter) effect on the film or camera sensor rather than a normally-made image. This is because cameras take pictures of reflected light (either ambient lighting or the flash). A corroboration of this phenomenon is thought to exist when the people present can't see the ghost and there's nothing in front of the camera that could be reflecting the light required to record an image. This is thought to be especially definite if a second camera does not record the same thing.

Polaroid, we hypothesized, was especially useful since it's "instant" (okay, not as instant as digital, but it *is* an older technology); the film has a very lengthy chemical process happening and we know from laboratory study of psychokinesis that affecting something moving or in process is potentially easier than affecting something fixed or motionless; and, finally, the camera itself is simple and not given to the kinds of flash reflections that digital and 35-mm cameras with more powerful flashes are—in other words, no orbs!

In addition, the Polaroid company has been very giving of its time looking at anomalous photos and giving expert opinions as to whether the effects are or are not explainable.

ANNETTE: [Moving through the kitchen] *What I feel is over here. I am getting goose bumps.*

LOYD: I took a couple of Polaroid shots, but nothing unusual came up on them. I pulled out my handy-dandy TriField EMF Meter and switched it on.

Not getting anything significantly magnetic in that area. No unanticipated fluctuations from the baseline, either.

ANNETTE: *Okay.*

LOYD: Annette walks into a storage or pantry area.

In the pantry area

ANNETTE: *Loyd, come in here, this room is very cold. Right there* [Pointing to the right]. *I have goose bumps everywhere. Yeah, I think this is an entrance, a portal. Still feels very cold here.*

I felt someone, maybe a man, walking up and down the corridor. There is movement in this hallway and in that other room. Do they tend to migrate towards electrical wiring?

LOYD: *We sometimes find that people can perceive things better when there is an energy source that is live. It may be an effect on the brain itself.*

We left the storage area, heading back to the large multi-purpose room.

ANNETTE: *It's very strong in there* [Referring to the storage room].

We reentered the large room where we had experimented with tossing the water bottle up into the rafters.

LOYD: *Do you think there is a history imprinted in this room?*

ANNETTE: *The main room that we passed when we first walked into the building has the most energy that I have felt so far. And when I went into the ladies room nearby, the toilet flushed by itself. Not the one I was in, but next to me.*

LOYD: *I can't tell you how many times I have gone to haunted restaurants where the ladies room is haunted. I can think of four right off the top of my head.*

The main room, which faces San Francisco Bay

I indicated we should move back to the main room, it had large windows looking out towards the bay. In front of the windows was a platform. Annette moved to the platform and windows.

ANNETTE: *What I felt was a lot of energy, right around here.*

LOYD: *Right here?*

I set down the TriField Meter as well as a Natural EMF meter, which measures non-tech sources of magnetic and EM fields. The latter meter has a sound indicator to alert the user when the readings change.

ANNETTE: *I am going to turn on my tape recorder and see if we can pick up any voices.* [Pauses] *Something is registering with me. When Maggie and I were talking earlier in here, we could smell cigarette smoke.*

LOYD: *Right here?*

ANNETTE: *Yes.*

I took a few deep breaths and began to channel. Loyd stood close and David continued to shoot video. Bruce, and Maggie stood a bit further away.

She stands at the window here, waiting for him. Ah, she's asking me why he hasn't come.

My name is Annette and this is Loyd and David. There is nothing to be afraid of. Can you show me something? I know that you can move things. Can you show me?

Annette contacting the apparition

LOYD: Annette was providing both sides of the conversation for our benefit, but sometimes it appeared the questions being asked—by both the entity, Anna Marie, as we eventually learned she was named, and by Annette—were left unsaid. But, at least at first, it seemed Anna Marie was asking Annette questions.

ANNETTE: Anna Marie was certainly curious, and I was getting her questions intuitively.

ANNA MARIE (through Annette): *Yes, I am from San Francisco. I went to school here. Yes, I was born here and I went to Catholic school, Notre Dame de Victoria and St. Gabriel's and Mercy High School.*

I had to laugh at the next question.

ANNA MARIE: *Did I like the nuns? Some of them. You spend time in the chapel* [At the Presidio]. *You feel good there. You want to run and play with the children, but sometimes they get frightened."*

LOYD: *What is your name?*

ANNE MARIE: *Anna Marie.*

LOYD: *What is your last name?*

ANNE MARIE: *Guiterrez.*

LOYD: *Where were you born?*

ANNE MARIE: *Not in this country. I came as a child. Travelled a long ways.*

Annette communicating with the ghost

LOYD: *How did you travel? What mean of transportation?*

ANNE MARIE: *Mother said by boat. Mother was beautiful. I can't find her.*

LOYD: *Are you looking?*

ANNE MARIE: *She's not here.*

LOYD: *Should she be?*

ANNE MARIE: *I came back to find her, but she is not here. None of them are here.*

LOYD: *Where did you come back from?*

ANNE MARIE: *I don't know. I don't know.*

LOYD: *Do you remember when you came back here?*

ANNE MARIE: *People, many parties ... noise ... people ... men ... no ladies. I use to swing on a tree.*

LOYD: *A tree here?* [Annette nods] *Were you married?*

ANNETTE: *She's turned away from me, she is very sad. She says others come here but not her love. Not her man. "Many ships, many ships."*

LOYD: *Annette, can you tell what she is wearing?*

ANNETTE: *Yes. She is wearing this long white dress, with something tied in the center. She has very long hair but there is something tied around her head. Like a white scarf.*

LOYD: *How old is she?*

ANNETTE: *Oh, she looks young, she could be twenty. She keeps changing, sometimes she looks younger and sometimes she looks older. But when she stands here she looks about twenty. This is where she is waiting for him.*

LOYD: *The man she loves?*

ANNETTE: *She says she called him Pugsy, but that wasn't his real name.*

LOYD: *What was his real name?*

ANNETTE: *She doesn't want to talk any more. Anna Marie, can you tell me his name? "It's too painful," she says. It's alright, it's alright, we will call him Pugsy.*

She's waiting for him. This was the place where they would come and meet. There was a big tree, a great big tree, with branches that go way up. He put a rope around a branch so that she could swing and they would laugh.

LOYD: *Is the tree still here?*

ANNETTE: *No, but the tree was here.*

She doesn't understand why all these people were here. [A big sigh] *She said that if she stays here maybe he will find her. She can't find him. "Silly people, noisy, no people like us."*

LOYD: *What year does she remember being here?*

ANNETTE (for Anna Marie): *I can't remember the year.*

ANNETTE: *She thinks 1776.*

This is 1996, Anna Marie. We come with love and we don't want you to be sad and you can leave if you want. [Annette takes in two deep breaths] *Okay, she ran away. She ran out. Wow!*

LOYD: *So, she's basically stuck here?*

ANNETTE: *She is stuck here, on her fixation on this man. And there was this tree, like a big oak tree, I saw it so clearly, and laughing and giggling.*

LOYD: *Do you think it was taken down to build this building?*

ANNETTE: *I forgot to mention that I felt closer to the water when I was talking to Anna Marie.*

Did anything register on the meter?

LOYD: *Yes, a couple of times while she was speaking through you.*

ANNETTE: *She would come in close to me and then she would back away. At one point it was like we were holding hands. She is very friendly, very loving, but also very sad.*

MAGGIE: *When Mary* [A friend of Maggie's] *came, she said she felt something in here. I told her that it's on the stage nearby where we always hear the thud, like a window being opened, but it is not. And one of the other girls feels something near this window.*

Conversing with Anna Marie's spirit

LOYD: *I don't consider myself psychic but, over the years I have become more sensitive. When we first entered the building, I felt I had to come over here. I felt something. But now I don't feel anything.*

ANNETTE: *Now she is gone. I didn't want to tell her that he is dead, because I don't have conclusive evidence to tell her. I didn't want to frighten her. But she can't find him.*

LOYD: *Except we can say for sure that he is dead if she was around a couple of hundred years ago.*

ANNETTE: *Yes, he is dead, but she can't find him.*

LOYD: *Because she is staying here?*

ANNETTE: *She can't find her mother either, because she is stuck here on Earth. It was interesting as she was looking at my clothes and we look so strange to her.*

LOYD: *When I asked her what year it was, I almost asked her to look out the window and tell us what she saw.*

ANNETTE: *What I felt were other longer wooden boats, when I looked out the window.*

LOYD: *Masted? With masts?*

ANNETTE: *Masted, yes, big boats. Oh, she said she wanted us to see the chapel. Let's see if there is any registration there.*

We all walked outside to see the excavation of the building next to the Officers' Club.

MAGGIE: *Underneath this building is a complete collapsed building.*

LOYD: *Is the chapel under here?*

MAGGIE: [Nodding] *This is the ante room, and the cross was found here in one of these holes.*

ANNETTE: *I think there are some graves under here, if they excavate underneath the building.*

LOYD: *I am getting some high readings on the meters.*

ANNETTE: *I think she comes over here to visit. Ok, poor darling, I feel so sorry for her.*

MAGGIE: *Such sadness.*

ANNETTE: *Yes, sadness, as she is so confused.*

We walked back into the Officers' Club building again and walked back to the bathrooms, where I had had my experience, and where Maggie had mentioned others had as well.

ANNETTE: *I didn't find a man here.*

MAGGIE: *Before, I have walked into this other bathroom and smelled cigar smoke.*

LOYD: *Annette, do you feel anything here?*

Again, I was getting anomalously high readings on my EMF sensors.

ANNETTE: *Really hot. If anyone is in here, can you flush the toilet? Can you turn the water on? I feel your presence.*

We waited a few minutes, but nothing happened.

Okay, he doesn't want to participate.

As we left the room, I felt a bit of relief.

I got really hot in there.

MAGGIE: *I got really cold while you were in here.*

LOYD: Most people associate cold spots with paranormal phenomena, but in most cases outside of Hollywood films and TV shows, the actual temperature does not change. It's the sensation of cold—like the cold chill one can experience when afraid or startled—that's being experienced. In this situation, Annette felt hot, and Maggie felt cold.

ANNETTE: Maggie also mentioned to me that she felt a man was around.

Remember when we were walking down around the kitchen and I felt something male in the hallway?

LOYD: *Yes, I think this is a residual energy of a male.*

We continued to talk as we headed out to Maggie's office, as Annette seemed tired and felt there was little else this time around.

I made note of one thing about the last male energy felt—let's face it, over the years there were many, many males here in the Officers' Club. That could be the residual energy of one of them or even one of their ghosts, or the residual energy of Anna Marie's lover.

Before we left, we discussed what had happened with Maggie, who felt good about Anna Marie's ghost being around, though we all acknowledged feeling a bit sorry for her. We then discussed returning in a few months with a slightly different purpose.

About a year later, in October of 1997, Annette and I conducted a full day seminar in the front room of the Presidio Officers' Club, videotaped by David Richardson. The seminar, which is available on DVD at www.mindreader.com, was essentially a one day session on conducting paranormal investigations, presenting the perspectives of the scientist and the psychic to balance the material.

We checked in for Anna Marie's presence while there that day, but there was no sign of her. Whether she had moved on (which we later found to be not so) or was simply elsewhere was not known to us. A shame, really, because it would have been great for the attendees to experience her a bit.

I put the Officers' Club into my files and thought little about it until a few years later when the Presidio became more welcoming to visitors, offering tours and renting space for events.

In 2002 I was approached by TechTV (now G4) to do a ghost hunting segment, and they had heard the Officers' Club was haunted. They were surprised to learn I'd actually been there before on an investigation, since they found no indication that anyone had done such a visit previously. Hey, when someone asks me for confidential, it stays confidential!

The segment aired in September, 2002, and was picked up by ABC News to run on *World News Now* the same month.

The Officers' Club was not the near empty building I'd visited previously, as it was now an active site for visitors and park personnel, with a café. Folks at TechTV found new witnesses, who were unaware of the activity previously reported to me.

Among the experiences reported by these witnesses was one of the café manager seeing, out of the corner of her eye, a man in a green uniform and a coat, which other people say they have seen too. Unexplained sounds of people moving about and other apparitions were also reported.

On my brief visit there for the shoot, it seemed that perhaps Anna Marie was also still with us. I stood in the same area in front of those windows on the San Francisco Bay as before and felt that same presence. I mentally asked that she indicate her presence by affecting my EMF meters.

Loyd checking for magnetic fields

As if on command, both meters spiked, and then fluctuated wildly. I thanked her (again, mentally), and both devices settled back down to a baseline reading.

Coincidence? I think not.

If you make it to the Presidio, which offers tours that sometimes mention the ghosts of the park (yes, there are other reportedly haunted sites in the Presidio), be sure to step into the Officers' Club and offer Anna Marie your greetings.

San Francisco Chinatown

A City Within a City

The Gate to Chinatown on Grant Street
(source: www.pachd.com)

A breathtaking, decorated Dragon's Gate to usher in good fortune, gloriously marks the entry to San Francisco's Chinatown: a city within a city, stretching along twenty-four blocks with elaborate 1920s-vintage streetlights sculpted as golden dragons lighting the way.

A San Francisco ghost guidebook would not be complete without including exotic Chinatown. You may think you've left America as you enter to hunt for tales of Chinatown's supernatural past and present. Come along as we journey through mysterious streets, narrow alleyways, restaurants and temples where the ghosts and spirits bide their time.

An estimated 30,000 people make their homes in Chinatown, the largest such community in the United States after New York's Chinatown. A majority of residents are either recent immigrants or first-generation Americans who still speak their native Cantonese or Mandarin dialect.

San Francisco actually got its start in Chinatown. In 1846, Captain John Montgomery rowed ashore with a small detachment of sailors and marines to raise the American flag at Portsmouth Square, at the heart of what is today's Chinatown, claiming the soon-to-be-renamed community as U.S. territory. Two years later, the square was the site of the announcement of the discovery of gold in the nearby Sierra foothills.

Thousands of Cantonese from Guangzhou and Hong Kong came to this corner of the world when gold was discovered. They planned to return to their homeland after striking it rich, but due to the deteriorating social conditions under China's ruling Manchu Dynasty many remained in North America, working on the railroads, laboring on the farms, fishing or opening small businesses.

LOYD: Annette has a real affinity for Chinatown. When she gave me her write-up of our visit to seek out any resident ghosts and residual haunts, I was struck by how her narrative really captured the spirit of our visit there.

So, Annette is going to tell you this story, with just a few interruptions from me, and a few comments after.

Making Contact with Chinatown

When we contacted the San Francisco Chinatown Ghost Tours, owner Cynthia Yee was excited to meet with us and discuss how we could incorporate our book with their tours. Yee is a well-known Bay Area personality, being a recipient of the Bay Area Jefferson Award, which recognizes people who do outstanding public service in the community. She is founder of the San Francisco-based Grant Avenue Follies.

It was appropriate for me to have found Chinatown-born Yee, given my own performing background, as she is a former dancer. At the age of nine, she was inspired by nightclub performer Dorothy Toy, the first Asian to be booked into the London Palladium.

Cynthia invited us to dim sum at the Four Seas Restaurant at 731 Grant Avenue, the oldest Chinese Restaurant in Chinatown, and, perhaps not so coincidentally, Loyd's favorite restaurant in that area.

LOYD: I have to say I was kind of blown away that the one restaurant in Chinatown that I've been going to since I first came to the Bay Area in 1979 was to be our meeting place.

ANNETTE: We ascended the giant black staircase into a red-velvet hallway lined with photos from the 1950s to today; snapshots of Martin Yan, Gavin Newsom, Willie Brown and a number of other celebrities including some presidential candidates. Passing the bar area, we entered the dining room. Murals of religious figures decorate the front and back walls. The atmosphere has a traditional elegance accented by artwork, Chinese pottery, and the traditional round tables covered with white table-cloths and graced with Chinese red napkins.

Brushed red velvet, outlined in gold, draped the large windows overlooking Grant Ave. I truly felt like I had stepped back into one of my favorite places on the planet, Hong Kong.

The hostess, wearing a traditional Chinese red and gold jacket, escorted us to the table near a window where Cynthia and her two companions, Russell, a retired international tour guide, and Chuck Gee, who was formerly the costume designer for the famed *Forbidden City Nightclub*, were seated. After the introductions we were treated to a delightful dim sum lunch.

LOYD: Let me reiterate how terrific the food is at Four Seas. Not just the dim sum, which you can get every day for lunch, but their regular menu as well. I've brought many friends there over the years, and never been disappointed.

ANNETTE: Loyd, a professional mentalist and former magician, was delighted and surprised to hear that Cynthia Yee was a magician and had just returned from a convention where she performed. Their discussion involved many mutual friends and acquaintances in the magic community.

As we finished the wonderful food, Cynthia asked if we would like to take a little tour of Chinatown and acquaint ourselves with their ghost tour. Of course we were ready, so off we went to discover a new world in this city within a city. We began our walk on Grant Street, which is the area's main commercial thoroughfare, running from Bush Street to Broadway, a distance of eight blocks. I couldn't help but admire all the lanterns and banners hanging across the street. Cynthia told us that red stands for happiness, green for longevity, and yellow for good fortune.

Our first stop was going to be the Empress of China roof garden restaurant, between Clay and Washington Streets. Chuck told us it was located on the sixth floor of an old building with a million-dollar view of the city.

The Empress of China building also houses many offices. Adjacent to the lobby elevators which would take us to the sixth floor were photos dating back thirty to forty years. Famous people including Jayne Mansfield, Erik Estrada, Sammy Davis Jr., Peter Lawford, Mick Jagger, Jackie Chan, Marcel Marceau, numerous well-known Asian actors and our current governor, Arnold Schwarzenegger were all represented. Even George H. W. Bush has eaten there.

As we stepped into the elevator, Cynthia told us that this roof garden retreat features the cuisine of all China in an opulent atmosphere of dynastic splendor and elegance. She said, "The interior reflects the beauty, color, and architectural form from the [206 BC] Han Dynasty."

Needless to say, I was anxious not only to see if we had a ghost here, but also to see the elegance of the Chinese of the past. The elevator opened and there in front of us was a magnificent silk embroidery. I have a passion for Chinese embroideries since I own what is probably the largest collection in the world of Mandarin sleeves and Mandarin squares (but that is another story!).

LOYD: I'd only been to the Empress of China once before, years ago. I can honestly say that walking in with Cynthia, Russell, and Chuck providing commentary gave me a real appreciation for what we were experiencing. And then there were Annette's perceptions....

ANNETTE: As we walked towards the atrium, Cynthia said, "There have been sightings of ghosts around the atrium, near the coat closet, and near the hostess desk, where the staff takes the reservations.

Chuck added: "But it hasn't been just once that they were sighted— it has been from time to time that people have seen things. Also, from the fifth floor area where the ladies restroom is located, there have been some sightings."

Cynthia told us that over forty years ago a Chinese man named Kee Joon and his partners planned out this elegant beauty. In 1966, Mao launched the Cultural Revolution. As if in answer to this outrage, Kee Joon opened the doors to the Empress, complete with silk brocade walls, antique palace chandeliers, temple artifacts, carvings of teak, striking portraits, ornate

Annette in the atrium

scrolls, and imperial peacock feathers, all representative of China's tradition and history.

The atrium was ornate, with a tree growing in the center and fresh green flowers lining the circumference, giving one the feeling of a lovely garden. I kept telling myself, "You have to concentrate Annette. You are not here to enjoy this great beauty but to look for ghosts." With my hands stretched out in front of me and Loyd on my right, we began to move towards the coat closet.

"Oh, I am getting goose bumps, there is some energy here near the coat closet," I whispered to Loyd. I asked him, "Do you feel that?"

"Yep," Loyd acknowledged.

LOYD: Indeed, I had felt a pressure of sorts, the kind I'm used to experiencing when something or someone of a more psychic nature is present.

ANNETTE: "There was a man that just went by very quickly," I said. "He saw me and I think I startled him. He was probably about 5 feet, 4 inches, on the thin side. The jacket he was wearing was the dark blue Mao jacket once so prevalent in China. He definitely had a long black queue down his back and something on his head. He was bowing his head so

Artist's conception of one of the ghosts

I wouldn't see him clearly, but I know that he saw me and felt that I was aware of his presence."

As I walked around the fountain toward the hostess desk, the energy felt normal, but just as I approached the desk I began to pick up energy again and my goose bumps became apparent. "Loyd, there is something over here." I motioned him over towards me. He stood next to me and I continued, "I am seeing two men this time, wearing the old Chinese coats and hats, queue down their backs, very Cantonese looking. They both look shorter than the other man and heavier, with round faces."

One of the men leaned forward towards me, almost about to say something and realized that I could see him. He turned to the other man and spoke, but I couldn't hear the words. Before I could say anything they both scurried away very quickly. "Oh, they seemed very shy."

Chuck said, "These must have been the former tenants who loved this place, decided to stay on, even though they built a new building here. I think they were a little afraid of Caucasians. Don't forget these were the

Artist's conception of the ghosts in the atrium

early settlers that came to San Francisco. They must have been here during the gold rush days, 1900s or so?"

"I would say that maybe in the late 1800s," I replied, "and they reminded me of some of the Chinese Cantonese men I saw in Hong Kong during the late 1960s."

Chuck said, "The queue were cut off after 1910 here in the U.S. Dr. Sun Yat-sen helped dethrone the royal family and had the men cut off their queue."

Russell motioned us over to the western window and said, "See that old brick building, the wide one? That is the YWCA building and the turret, the north tower, has a woman ghost."

"Do you think we could get into that building," I asked.

Cynthia said we might be able to at some later date.

We continued down the stairs to the mezzanine, where the restrooms were located.

As I entered the ladies room alone, the door squeaked ominously, just like the inner sanctum in a scary movie, where something horrible was going to either grab at or try to stab the heroine. Taking a deep breath, with my Olympus tape recorder in hand, I proceeded ahead and closed the door, hoping to pick up any energies.

LOYD: Okay—yet another haunted ladies' room in another haunted restaurant!

ANNETTE: The entry room was smallish and decorated with red velvet wallpaper. Two porcelain sinks encased in a beautifully carved rosewood cabinet were on the east side of the room, and a small table and chair were near the west wall. I spoke out loud, "Ok, now I am in the ladies room. Is there anyone in here?" There wasn't an answer, but I got a cold chill as I moved toward the bathroom stalls on the north side of the second room.

"Oh, ok," I sighed. I had just encountered an invisible wall…that, oh-so-familiar invisible wall that tells me immediately that I have walked into a residual haunting, a traumatic moment in time that leaves an indelible impression on the building or area.

I spoke into my recorder, "What I am seeing is a Chinese man lying on a bed. The room is small, like a small bedroom. Seems to be very dark, just one window on the north wall. He seems to be very ill. I think he is dying. He raised up a bit from the bed and then went back down, several times."

I exited the ladies room and told our group what I had encountered. Continuing on with how I felt, I announced, "So, my feeling is that there are a great many impressions still in this building, even though they tore down the original building and built the new one over it years ago."

"Yes, so much history here," Loyd chimed in. "More than much of San Francisco." Loyd went on to explain to our tour guides about residual hauntings—that they seem to be a recording of a past emotional event. As they are often repetitive in nature, speaking with the "ghosts" in a residual haunting tends to do no good because they just continue to go about their business.

"A good example is Gettysburg, the battle field in Pennsylvania. It has repetitive stuff, but there are no actual ghosts there. It's a recording of parts of the actual battle that people are picking up on," Loyd explained.

Chuck asked, "They are not here to scare people?"

"No, no, not to scare anyone," Loyd answered.

Chuck continued, "It is their territory, they like this place?"

I answered Chuck's question, "With an impression, it is definitely their energy that has been left, but nothing intelligent."

"But what about the guys upstairs?" Loyd asked.

"They were definitely ghosts. They were scurrying around and definitely saw me, definitely ghosts!" I said emphatically.

"So in their case, they are following a habitual pattern to be here, just like the pattern of people walking a certain way to get to work, to go to a certain place, yet still able to react to outside stimuli," Loyd added.

Laughing, I replied, "Yes, and they were reacting to me. I scared them!"

"You were invading their space," Chuck said almost apologetically.

"Yes, well, they weren't expecting me to be able to see them," I laughed.

Chuck told us that the building was an apartment tenement house, "mostly filled with Chinese men, except for one Caucasian piano teacher. Some blond lady. I think she was the only Caucasian lady as all the rest of them didn't speak English."

With that, we left the Empress of China and began walking through Chinatown.

Our next stop was the Imperial Restaurant at 818 Washington Street, between Grant Avenue and Waverly Place.

Once we arrived at the restaurant, Chuck said that a massacre had taken place here on September 4, 1977. It was known as the Golden Dragon Restaurant at the time. He explained he couldn't go inside because it made him sick to his stomach, but that we had to see this restaurant because, to him, there was definitely something imprinted there.

Chuck filled us in a bit on the history. "There had been a long standing feud between two rival Chinese gangs, Wah Ching and the Joe Boys. At 2:40 in the morning it came to a head when a botched assassination attempt by the Joe Boys at the Golden Dragon Restaurant killed five people, including two tourists, and injured eleven people, none of whom were gang members."

Cynthia chimed in, "Due to this Golden Dragon Massacre, the San Francisco Police Department created the Asian Gang Task Force. Five men from the Joe Boys were arrested and convicted for the crime and three are still in prison."

"Well, let's see what we can find," I sighed.

As soon as we walked through the entryway of the Imperial Palace restaurant, we felt that familiar wall of energy, except this time it was the heaviest that I have ever felt. "Extremely heavy in here, extremely heavy energy," I whispered to Loyd.

"Yes, whoa, it's heavy," he replied trying to catch his breath.

LOYD: I felt an incredible heaviness, and a real sense of pressure and even disgust. I'd only experienced that in a few other places, including a cell in Alcatraz. I had a hard time moving into the place, and really empathized with what Chuck had reported feeling.

ANNETTE: Loyd stayed in the foyer as I walked towards the back of the restaurant, trying to act as if I belonged in there as a customer. Every table was filled with little plates and the waiters were bustling around with their dim sum carts, shouting out what they were selling. The noise level was unbearable, with everyone trying to talk over everyone else.

I tried to tune out the noise and walked towards the kitchen to see if I could pick up any ghostly activity, but the more I walked, the more it was difficult to breathe. I looked to see if anyone was there who wanted to talk to me, but couldn't see anything.

Then, out of the corner of my eye, I saw some bodies running towards the kitchen, which is on the north side of the room. They disappeared back there. They didn't feel like ghosts though; more like something from another residual haunting.

I headed back to the foyer to find Loyd a little pale and still trying to catch his breath. He said that he could feel the bad energy right where he was standing and it was overwhelmingly heavy and hard to breath. "Let's get out of here," he said quietly.

"Yes, I feel the same way. This is just one gigantic impression of death, definitely residual energy. This is worse than being in one of the cells at Alcatraz," I told him.

Once outside with the rest of the group the feeling of oppression began to slide away from my body and mind. We described our encounter in the restaurant and Cynthia and Chuck both agreed that they choose not to eat at the restaurant as it is too uncomfortable for them.

LOYD: Yet it was clear that lots of people did not experience what we did, and the people in the crowded restaurant seemed to be enjoying their food. I would never warn people away from the Imperial Palace, as that would be quite unfair to the place, especially since we were told the food was quite good.

ANNETTE: Chuck told us that they have had several people come in to exorcise the building.

Loyd said, "But perhaps they exorcised the ghost, but not the bad energy, that still lingers here."

I told them about the kitchen area and what I saw.

Cynthia said, "Yes, that is the area where a fellow named Raymond Chow was sitting when they started firing their guns, that's who they were after. He and his men ran out the back of the kitchen."

"Wow, well, that residual impression is still very strong in there!" I replied.

We followed Cynthia back into the street and began walking.

Ross Alley

We headed toward Ross Alley, which we were told is San Francisco's oldest alley, off of Washington Street near Grant. It was known at one time for its brothels, gambling houses, and opium dens that sprang up to cater to men far from home, effectively sequestered in the overcrowded "Chinese Quarter."

Ross Alley is a very narrow throughway that has retained enough of its character to double for other locations in motion pictures, such as *Indiana Jones and the Temple of Doom.*

Tourists cluster in front of the fortune cookie factory, where some 20,000 fortune cookies a day are handmade by two women, each manning a conveyor belt of what look like miniature waffle irons. The factory

In Ross Alley

opened in August 1962, and though there are other fortune cookie baker-
ies in the city and this is not the company's main location, it's the only one
where the cookies are still made by hand, the old-fashioned way.

You will find locals toting pink bags for groceries and see laundry hung
out to dry on the fire escapes high above the storefronts. You'll see signs for
acupuncture, the Lim Family Benevolent Society, and ninety-eight cent
merchandise. This is Ross Alley.

Ross Alley is where, early in December 1875, a prostitute named Xijiao
was slaughtered in her room. Although Xijiao was just one among hundreds of Chinatown prostitutes at the time, she was one of the best-known.

Chuck pointed above our heads. "We are looking up at two decks made
out of metal above the Christian mission. The girls would come out onto
the balcony to entice the sailors to come up and see them. But several of
the girls met their death by falling over the balconies."

Taking in a deep breath and focusing on the windows, I began to see
someone looking at me. I pointed to something moving in the far right
window. "Loyd, I keep getting something up here in the windows, definitely in the window. Yes! I'm seeing a girl, that looks like she is around
sixteen years old, long black hair. She is moving and ah, I get the name
Ping Lee! First name is Ping."

Chuck said, "Ping, means 'peace', and her surname could have been
Ping."

"There is definitely one girl, and she is a ghost and she says her name is
Ping Lee," I repeated.

"The only problem is that we cannot get into that building, as it is rented
to a family," Cynthia informed us.

"Yes, too bad, as she wants to talk to me and help her leave," I replied.

We continued through Chinatown and were led to the Chinese Hospital.

Cynthia gave us an overview of the place: "Here we are, at the Chinese
Hospital on Jackson St. above Stockton St. It was erected in 1924. Often
times when people were diagnosed with a terminal illness in the olden
days, there was no family here because of the bachelor society. And also
many did not have medical care, so they ended their lives by either hangings or jumping out of the windows on this side of the building. They
would find the body in the alley."

Loyd and I walked down the narrow alleyway but couldn't pick up anything, which is perhaps not surprising since there were no witnesses to
ghostly happenings at the hospital.

"Probably there would be more energy inside the hospital," Loyd commented, "as there often is in many hospitals."

"Yes, I agree, but certainly nothing like we just experienced at the restaurant! Wow, that was something else."

We walked back to the sidewalk and the rest of the group and relayed that all was quiet, nothing there.

Quong Ming Jade Emperor Palace

Cynthia suggested we next go to a temple a block away called the Quong Ming Jade Emperor Palace, located at 1123 Powell Street, between Jackson and Washington Streets.

As we came upon the temple, Cynthia stated, "This is the time that the Gates of Heaven are open, so this is a good time to visit."(In Chinese tradition, the seventh month in the lunar calendar is regarded as the Ghost Month, during which ghosts and spirits, including those of deceased ancestors, come out from the lower realm to visit the living. On the fifteenth day of the month the realms of Heaven, Hell and that of the living open.)

Chuck bowed to a gentleman sitting in a small room off to the left as we entered the beautiful temple. "This is the priest, Annette and Loyd."

We moved inside and saw several women folding silver paper that was clearly meant to be symbolic of something. "They are folding the silver bars for the ancestors," Cynthia told us.

We walked towards the back of the temple into a room with small plaques with photos and names in Chinese. Chuck explained, "They have pictures of their ancestors," referring to the plaques. "They have the photos so you can see them."

As we moved out of the back room, Chuck continued. "The primary thing in a Chinese temple is the burning of incense. We believe that the smoke carries the prayers to heaven."

I began opening my perceptions to see what I would pick up. "I keep getting glimpse of a very small woman. Hmm, getting an impression, a very small woman, kind of stout. She was over there on the right side of the altar and then disappeared. Very fleeting, can't get her again. I am going to walk over to the altar again," I told Loyd.

Loyd leaned over and said, "Just an impression? Yes, that makes sense for a place like this."

Cynthia joined Loyd as I walked back and said, "Ok, I saw her again, but very faint." Turning to Cynthia, I asked "Do they ever put flowers on the altar?"

Cynthia nodded her head yes.

"Because I saw this tiny older woman," I told her, "arranging flowers on the right side of the altar and then walking over and putting them on the altar. She has a very loving energy, but definitely an impression. A nice feeling, very spiritual person. A good feeling."

I announced that the whole building has a wonderful loving presence.

Chuck said, "Well, Cynthia's mother, Mildred Fong, is the high priestess. She is 91 and runs this temple. When Cynthia was little, her mother, who was born here and speaks English, translated for all the neighbors who needed forms and applications filled out."

LOYD: The temple was not a place I would expect would have much activity, unless of course the spirits of the ancestors did come back to worship with their descendents. It was a very peaceful yet ornate place, and I thanked Cynthia for sharing this with us.

St. Louis Place Alley

ANNETTE: We continued back down Jackson Street to St. Louis Place Alley. As we arrived and peered down the alley, Chuck told us, "This is where the slave trade went on."

"Well, I am getting goose bumps. Are you feeling anything," I asked Loyd.

LOYD: To be honest, I was not experiencing anything out of the ordinary. But then, I'm the parapsychologist, not the psychic.

ANNETTE: We both started to walk down the narrow alley. About three-quarters of the way down, I shouted, "Oh, right here, there must be a tunnel here, I see them shuffling young girls back and forth. I get a lot of prostitution, lots of fear in these young girls." I was struck with a profound sense of sadness.

"Yeah, that's what Chuck said. The slave trade, that's what they were sold for," confirmed Loyd.

"Just impressions, Loyd, but no ghosts. These scared young girls," I continued.

We walked back to the group and I felt like I had stepped back in a time tunnel, seeing these young faces, so desperate and scared.

I explained what I picked up and asked Cynthia another question, "Is there a tunnel underneath here?"

Chuck responded, "We definitely have hidden tunnels in the area. We helped collaborate on a screen play on that sort of thing. These young woman were quite valuable, at least $10,000 to buy up their contract. They were under bondage and brought in by the Tong. They went to China to

St. Louis Place Alley

secure these girls on the pretense they were going to get them employment in America. They would lie to the impoverished parents, saying, 'She will not have to starve. She will be well-treated.' They would tell the families that the girls would be able to get money to help support them. But it was all a lie. They were treated like slaves." Cynthia added in reference to the perceived tunnel, "You can walk into any one of these buildings and go into the basement and walk all the way down to Grant Avenue."

"This is a community where people are still engaged," Chuck said. "That's why preserving Chinatown—keeping it a community where people will live and not just a tourist attraction—is very important spiritually."

LOYD: We decided we had spent enough time for the day, as Annette was getting tired (okay, I admit it—me, too). We headed down the street and said our good-byes.

To me, Chinatown is both a source of immense history and culture for San Francisco. That there has been so much happiness coupled with so much misery since its founding makes for an especially fertile ground for residual haunting.

But clearly, based on both witnesses' experiences and Annette's perceptions, there are places where more than a few ghosts may congregate, still going through the motions from their long-ago lives, yet fully aware—albeit sometimes surprised—that the living can sometimes see them.

As we moved through the different locations in Chinatown, the ubiquitous tool of the ghost hunter, my EMF meter, did pick up some anomalous readings in a few places, notably when Annette was perceiving the apparitions at the Empress of China. A high reading was also associated with the big energy we experienced due to the psychic impression at the Imperial Palace. Other locations brought minor fluctuations.

But to be honest, as a parapsychologist I know that the sensor readings have little meaning without connection to the experience of people. It's much more interesting to hear what a psychic practitioner like Annette has to say and how what she says relates to history and to the experiences of other witnesses.

I look forward to my next visit to Chinatown, though that may be for more dim sum than to look for more ghosts.

One additional interesting note: Our visit took place around the "Festival of the Hungry Ghosts," held the fifteenth day of the seventh Moon (usually in August). According to our guides, desperate and angry ghosts must be placated, and the only way to avoid their mischievous doings and hate is to offer sacrifices to them, essentially to buy them off. But just as families do not invite beggars and strangers inside the house, these souls are not encouraged to enter, and sacrifices to them are made outside the home. A Taoist temple or gravesite is the norm.

Alcatraz: Escape to the Haunted Island

San Francisco Bay

Approaching Alcatraz Island (courtesy David Richardson)

Known the world over as "The Rock," this fortress imprisoned the worst of the worst. Over a million tourists visit each year, but few have this chance to explore the hidden citadel under the cellblock, retrace the steps of the most daring escapes or visit the cell of the famous birdman of Alcatraz.

—From "Alcatraz Revealed," a Travel Channel production featuring
Annette and Loyd

ANNETTE: In the fall of 2003, Loyd and I were hired by The Travel Channel to explore the famous Alcatraz Prison for hidden ghosts. Believe it or not, I was born and raised in San Francisco, and in all those years had never ventured out to the infamous prison. To me, the fog-enshrouded island, with its cold, damp winds, watery isolation, and forbidding past of housing evil souls, loomed out of the Bay uninvitingly.

My anxiety was running high at the thought of going into this prison and perhaps running into one of those evil souls that had not passed into the light. There had been many murder cases that I had worked on before this trip, but they were individuals, certainly not numbering the more than 1,557 men who the records show passed through the gates of Alcatraz as prisoners. Public enemies No. 1, murderers, rapists, mafia associates, kidnappers, thieves, notorious criminals all. Oh my!

Local Native Americans have believed that the island was an evil place, as it has seen centuries of death from murders, suicides, and unexplained accidents. With this dark past, it's no wonder Alcatraz is said to be one of the most haunted places in the nation.

Throughout the years guards, prisoners, visitors, and National Park service employees have reported mysterious happenings on Alcatraz Island. There are a multitude of stories, from cell doors mysteriously closing to soldiers appearing in front of startled guards, guests, and family members who were living on the island. It even seems that the original lighthouse reappears on occasion. Torn down after being damaged in the great 1906 San Francisco earthquake, it is said it will suddenly appear and a whistling sound can be heard all over the island.

The following is part of a letter that Felicia Fowler-Alexander sent to me on February 26, 2009, as a result of my request to her to send me any stories she might have about ghosts on Alcatraz. Felicia worked on Alcatraz in the book stores for more than three years, and I met her and her husband, Jason Alexander, through a mutual friend:

Several people I know had small to significant things happen. One of the Park Rangers—Benny—was chaperoning a group of Boy Scouts for an overnight on the island and he decided to sleep in the Birdman's cell up in the hospital. He said he was awakened by an overwhelming feeling of someone pushing down hard on his chest, like they were trying to pin him down. And Benny is one of those guys you sincerely believe, because he wouldn't probably even mention it if it weren't coerced out of him.

And then several people have mentioned seeing the image of a military soldier in Building 64 at the dock level of the island (it is labeled Residential Apartments on your diagram, but it was originally military cannon and ammunition casements, so definitely a logical place for him to be wandering around).

Eric, a security guard … would be a good person to talk to about that. He is ex-Marine, covered with tattoos … and one day when we were getting off the boat in the morning and he was just ending his overnight shift, he was as pale as could be and shaking … and he confessed to us what he saw (the same soldier ghost others had seen). He was sincerely "freaked out." This is the kind of guy that would never admit to being scared unless something truly happened to him that he couldn't shake.

And so we were going to investigate and see for ourselves if there were actually any real ghosts on The Rock!

LOYD: While not born and bred in the Bay Area (I'm from the New York area), I could certainly relate to Annette not having visited Alcatraz. I never went up to the top of the Empire State Building until I was in my mid-20s, and only then because a friend was visiting from California.

Until the Travel Channel show, I'd not been to Alcatraz since moving out here in 1979. However, I had visited a supposedly haunted prison in Darwin, Australia, with a Japanese TV crew and a Japanese medium named Aiko Gibo in the 1990s.

A Brief History of Alcatraz

ANNETTE: A royal Spanish ship-of-war captained by the Spanish explorer Juan Manuel de Ayala entered San Francisco Bay in the fall of 1775. Logs kept noted this island as a barren white rock. The white was caused by hundreds of pelican droppings, and they named it "Isla de los Alcatraces"—Island of the Pelicans, although Alcatraz refers to albatross in some versions.

In 1847, the island was taken over by the United States military and by 1853 a military fortress was being built. Within a year they had built the first lighthouse on the Pacific Coast here. Several years later a military prison was built on the island and Alcatraz had its first prisoners—court-martialed military convicts.

In 1907, Alcatraz became an official Army prison, and soon held both convicted Army members as well as German seamen who became prisoners of war in World War One. In 1934, the Military decided to close the prison due to the high cost of operation, and ownership was turned over to the Department of Justice.

Prohibition and the Great Depression of the late 1920s and 1930s created a new era of organized crime. Our nation was vulnerable to violent crimes with poverty running rampant and illegal booze smuggling becoming a force to be reckoned with. Influential mobsters and sharply-dressed public enemies affected life in metropolitan cities. Law enforcement was often ill-equipped to deal with the murders, crimes, gang shoot-outs, and other public slayings.

FBI Director J. Edgar Hoover, along with Attorney General Homer Cummings, waged war against the era's gangsters. Together they convinced the government that a "super-prison" was needed. Thus, on January 1, 1934, incarceration at Alcatraz became the maximum penalty for crime—short of execution. The island became famous for housing the most violent, relentless, and predatory criminals of the era.

Among the first groups of inmates were felons such as Arthur "Doc" Barker (who was the last surviving member of the Ma Barker Gang), George "Machine Gun" Kelly, Floyd Hamilton (a gang member and driver for Bonnie and Clyde), and Alvin "Creepy" Karpis. One of the most famous mobsters, convicted of tax evasion as a last, prosecutorial resort, was also incarcerated there: Al "Scarface" Capone.

Other inmates included Roy Gardner, last of the Old West train robbers; "Bumpy" Johnson, the Godfather of Harlem; and Morton Sobell, convicted in the Rosenberg espionage case; and the man who became famous as the "Birdman of Alcatraz," the violent criminal Robert Stroud.

Stroud was later immortalized by actor Burt Lancaster in *The Birdman of Alcatraz* film as a kindly bird lover. But in actuality, Stroud was a homicidal sociopath whom one longtime Alcatraz officer likened to "Jekyll and Hyde."

I remember my folks talking about one of the attempted escapes in 1946, where three inmates and two guards were killed.

LOYD: I knew some of the history of Alcatraz, and boned up a bit before we headed out to the island. I also knew that after it had been closed as a prison in 1963, it was occupied by a group of Native Americans (1969–1971), and there are tales that a group of Hell's Angels also occupied The Rock for a short period, although it was likely it was other bikers, who had been used as some form of security. However, it's been a National

Alcatraz Island (pachd.com)

Park open to the public since 1973 with more than one million visitors to the island every year.

ANNETTE: Along with Office of Paranormal Investigations member and videographer David Richardson, who had gotten permission to take still photos for us on this venture, Loyd and I met the production crew at Fisherman's Wharf, Pier 33, around 2:00 P.M. and boarded the Alcatraz ferry that carries thousands of tourists a month across the bay. It was chilly and slightly overcast. We drank hot coffee to warm us up a bit on the brief voyage.

By the time we all had finished our drinks we were ready to disembark onto this forbidding twenty-five-acre island. The ferry was filled with tourists excited about coming to this famous prison, a place where strange things can and do happen to this day.

I disembarked and walked around the landing area but didn't feel anything.

Several of the camera men and a producer were already on the island shooting around the tourists as much as they could. Loyd, David, and I were accompanied by one of the other producers, who had arranged for a small truck to drive us up the steep hill on an old service road.

A model of Alcatraz

On the left hand side of the road near the top we sighted the Warden's' house, which is a crumbling ruin. There are stories that it is haunted by an unknown ghost that was spotted by guards who were playing cards there many years ago. The ghost was said to have pulled out a deck of cards and started to "flip them" down like a "professional dealer." The guards immediately fled the house.

LOYD: Maybe they were more afraid of what the ghost would want as a pay-off in case they lost!

ANNETTE: One of the park rangers who escorted us up the road to the cell block told us a story about a mass sighting in the 1950s outside of the administrative office by a woman office worker and the warden's wife, who was hanging out clothes. According to the women, about sixty civil war soldiers appeared along the shore line along with the boom of cannons—in keeping with The Rock's history as a military fort during the Civil War era.

Another old story, told by one of the prison guards, involved another card game. He and several other guards had gone to the warden's house where a Christmas party was in full swing. Several of the them went into the back of the house and started playing poker where they witnessed a chilling apparition. Around midnight, as they played their last round of cards, a man wearing a gray, double-breasted suit and a hat with a brim—the kind a poker dealer wears—materialized out of thin air. He had mutton-chop side burns and a cigar hung out of the right corner of his mouth. One of the guards who had leaned back to exhale smoke from his own cigar saw the apparition and almost fell out of his chair.

When the ghost appeared, they noticed a drop in the temperature and a sudden chill in the room. Within seconds, the fire in the Ben Franklin stove was extinguished. Then the lights flickered off and on several times. They all knew it was time to go and quickly left the warden's house. After a night's sleep, the talk of the entire island was about the ghostly presence in the warden's residence. One can only assume that the warden and his family were either unaware of the ghost, or they simply accepted it as part of the household.

LOYD: These stories were of the days when Alcatraz was still a functioning prison, with guards and their families living on the island next to the prison. These days, other than the Rangers stationed there, and of course the tourists coming to visit, there's little "living" happening on the island—which makes for a desolate place for ghosts to want to hang out.

ANNETTE: You can't go into the warden's house anymore, as it is in ruins. It was disappointing that we couldn't investigate it ourselves and see if the ghost was still present. If he was, we might have had the ghost appear and tell me who he was.

Within a few minutes we reached the top and there before us stood the awesome Alcatraz cellhouse.

This huge cellhouse has four cell blocks. Each block is made of three tiers of individual cages with catwalks (like a porch running around the outside of each level). These are cell blocks A, B, C and D. All are inside the same four walls.

But D block, for the tough boys, had been somewhat separated. A concrete wall running the length of the building makes a separate room.

The gun gallery is two levels of barred catwalk, stuck on the side of the wall. It runs crossways to the cell blocks, across the building. Walking up and down, the gun guard can look down each corridor and help any floor guard in trouble. The gun gallery cannot be entered from inside the cell house. Guards go in from outside the building through a double set of steel doors. No guard ever went into the cell-house with a gun. They were up in the gun gallery.

The cameras were ready to roll and began with shots of Loyd and I walking around outside the cement patio. Then came the announcement: "It's time to go in!" I took a deep breath and glanced over at Loyd. He smiled and nodded his head. People were milling around taking photos, talking and laughing, when the sun began to peek out of the fluffy white clouds overhead.

We stepped inside the door as one of the tour groups was just leaving. The feeling of metal and concrete gave me a sense of the life shared in this place, a life that was always stark and gray. Some of the exiting visitors had smiles and others looked perplexed, apparently contemplating what they had encountered within, so I felt a little unnerved and wondered what where we really walking into.

LOYD: My own experience of walking in there was of intense curiosity, coupled with a bit of trepidation. As to the former, I was very interested to learn if there were truly so many conscious entities around as others before had stated there were, or if they had been misled by what should be an incredible set of residual hauntings and psychic impressions. My trepidation was based on my other prison experience in Australia, where there were no active apparitions, but there was a very heavy, sad, and depressed impression that was often tough to take.

Granted, I had a bit of a bias here. I did not expect there to be ghosts. Why would anyone, after death, want to hang around a prison? But a residual haunting? Absolutely. Then again, I've been wrong before about such things.

ANNETTE: I immediately became very aware of the smells that were in the building, a sort of musty, damp smell, very unusual, since the doors were open and I could feel the breezes going through the building. As we stepped further in, sounds echoed through the cell blocks, and one could imagine the din of a slamming cell door with the existing acoustics.

The Prison (pachd.com)

The prisoners nicknamed the long walkways between the cell blocks. The central walkway was Broadway and the others were named Park Avenue and Michigan Avenue. The area in between the mess hall and the cell blocks was called Times Square. The producer ushered us down Michigan Avenue, which is on the far right side, and stopped us at A Block. There were still some tours going through and she wanted to make sure that we were alone as we moved down to B Block. Loyd and David had to unpack all of their equipment.

LOYD: I'd brought along the two different EMF meters I typically use, a standard and a natural TriField meter, along with a digital thermometer, Polaroid and 35-mm cameras, and a simple static electricity detector. David had both a small digital video camera and a couple of still cameras.

ANNETTE: The producer, Tiffany Guichard, took the opportunity to ask us a few questions while we were waiting.

TIFFANY: *What kind of things do you feel people will pick up in Alcatraz?*

LOYD: *People can pick up all sorts of things in a haunted area. Annette can probably address that better.*

ANNETTE: *I feel that people, just a normal person, might feel cold or chills or tingling or the hair on the back of their neck raising. Some might get scared. A person who is sensitive may even pick up what had happened or feel that a tragedy had occurred in this place or room. Someone super sensitive, like myself, will begin to see the video play out the scene in full color as to what had happened there, and sometimes can even hear the conversation that went on in that room.*

TIFFANY: [Turning to Loyd with a quizzical look on her face] *How do you use Annette in your investigations?*

LOYD: *Annette is very sensitive to the environment on a very different level than most human beings. Many other people have the aptitude to develop that sensitivity, if they took the time and allowed their non-sensory perceptions to be noticed.*

I look at her experiences—what she perceives from the environment—and how they compare to those of any other witnesses. I use the technology, the other tools, to pick up any other physical components that can correlate to her experiences. But human experience is the most important piece. Technology means absolutely nothing without context, since none of it is or can be at this time designed to detect the psychic or paranormal in the environment. That's what human beings have as part of our design, and that is what Annette provides.

TIFFANY: *Annette, what do you do to prepare yourself for an investigation?*

ANNETTE: *The very first thing that I do is cover myself in White Light for protection, and I always wear my cross. I take a deep breath and we start walking. I use my hands, putting them in front of me like dowsing rods as I am*

One of the cell blocks

moving through buildings, and then I am able to pick up subtle energies, if there are energies there. Generally I am able to tell the difference between an impression and a ghost. That is the most important thing to do in our research, is deciding which is which, as most people think that they have a ghost but in actuality they only have an impression, which is the replay of an emotional event.

One of the sensations that I experience that is the most important when I get a hit are my goose bumps. They will go down my arms and legs, even reaching over my entire body and sometimes even on my face. Then I know immediately that I have hit on something that could possibly be a ghost or an impression. From there I go and decide which it is by what is happening there and whether or not I can contact the ghost. If I can contact the ghost, they generally will start to talk to me and I can begin to have a conversation with them. Impressions will not speak to me as they are just a video stuck in the atmosphere, and I will see the same scenario being played over and over again.

Tiffany smiled and asked what Loyd does as we move along in our investigations.

LOYD: [Turning his head to Annette] *I will ask Annette questions along the way when she gets her goose bumps and try to focus her attention and perceptions. And I try to get environmental sensor readings to compare against those perceptions.*

Annette felt apprehensive when first entering the cell blocks

ANNETTE: [Laughing] *Yes, things like, what are you seeing, what's happening, what's going on? That's how we work in tandem, it works very well!*

At this point the director had come up to ask a few questions. He told us that he had seen quite a few of our appearances on television shows and he had "found it so interesting that when Loyd asks Annette questions, she never gets disturbed or jarred. As a team you are really dialed in. When he is asking you questions you just talk about what you are experiencing, so naturally."

LOYD: I thanked him and said:

There are many other psychics who are on television that go into a seeming psychic trance but the reality is that psychic experience is part of normal experience. In Annette's case it is part of her normal experience, it's not something special for her, so when talking to her and asking her questions it's no different than a normal conversation.

ANNETTE: *Yes, exactly. I can hear him talking to me and I just keep moving along with the energy as I am walking. I am picking things up and telling him what I am seeing, what I am perceiving, what is going on. If someone, like a ghost, is talking to me, I let him know what they are saying, what they look like, what time period it was that they were alive. He is continually asking me questions. What we are doing actually is weaving a story on what we have discovered. And that's what makes it so exciting for us!*

LOYD: *Indeed, so let's begin and see what we can find.*

ANNETTE: Loyd, David, and I were ready to encounter any of those things that go bump in the day or night. With all equipment in hand, TV cameras ready to go, we continued down to Times Square, which is the far end of B Block.

As we turned the corner, I began to pick up a picture of a group of soldiers congregated against a door and stairway. It looked like five men. They were being beaten and kicked and punched and I saw men standing in front of them with rifles that had a piece of wood on the top of the them.

Loyd said it sounded like it must be an old gun from the 1800s. I agreed. It felt different and Loyd speculated that this might have been an impression from the time that Alcatraz was a Civil War installation. Loyd's EMF meters were really going crazy in this spot; he was getting some high readings at this point. I was covered in goose bumps and my body felt very heavy, like I had traveled way back in time.

LOYD: Many of us have noted the more consistent correlations with EM fields are between stationary high magnetic fields and residual impressions.

Annette, tell me more. What else are you experiencing?

ANNETTE: I tried to talk with the soldiers, intuitively and out loud, but got no response, so I knew for sure that they were not ghosts. This was definitely an impression, a residual haunting.

Tiffany was just standing with her mouth open at what we were experiencing and was upset that we'd started before they had their cameras running. The main director and cameramen were down in C Block waiting for us. But David was clicking away with his still camera.

LOYD: TV crews sometimes seem to think that nothing happens when the cameras aren't rolling. Or that we should "save it" for when they are. Unfortunately, as with so many things in life, psychic phenomena and experiences happen without the need for a director around to shout "Action."

ANNETTE: We were asked to move on to C Block, where they were waiting with cameras and lights. We turned left at the corner of Times Square and Seedy Street, which housed C Block, and I noticed that there were no tour groups around. As a matter of fact, it was quiet. Very quiet.

The director told the camera man to start shooting, and then asked Loyd and I to just walk down C Block and investigate.

There were two cell doors open on the left-hand side and I started to get the feeling that we needed to go into one of those two cells. With my hands outstretched in front of me, Loyd on my right, I felt compelled to go into a particular cell—cell C-104—which was quite small, maybe five feet wide by nine or ten feet long. There was a toilet and a small porcelain sink in the back of the cell and a fold-up bunk against the right hand wall. Glancing at the walls of this tiny room, it was noticeable that the paint was peeling with patches of off-white stucco showing through in many places.

As we entered, I moved towards the left hand side of the cell and almost immediately had to lean my back against the wall as my stomach began to churn.

[Moaning] *Oh, my God. This is bad! I have the sense that someone or several people have been murdered here! The smell of blood, lots of blood, is heavy in the air and I can hear men moaning. This is definitely an impression, not ghosts. I am covered with goose bumps.*

Loyd stared at me and immediately began to move his meter around, first on the ceiling, then on the floor and walls. He kept moving his meters to see if he could pick up any readings.

LOYD: I used the standard TriField EMF meter—can't move around the natural version the same way as the very movement causes a false reading. I was getting a different reading than outside the cell or in areas adjacent to that cell. I pointed the device toward the wall that Annette had just leaned up against.

We are getting a higher reading right here, getting a stationary field here.

ANNETTE: *I feel like a human being pinned against the wall. A lot of moaning. I just have this feeling of being crowded in this small cell, like there were quite a few people in here.*

That is very strange, why would there be so many people in here? And I keep hearing this moaning and blood!

LOYD: *Can you tell me how many people and who they are?*

ANNETTE: *They are either guards or inmates. I can't tell. The energy is very strong and I feel life being poured out of them, with blood, blood every-where. I keep seeing specks of blood on the walls, like they had been shot and the blood spattered and lots of blood on the floor!*

But, Loyd, this is definitely an impression, as I am trying to talk to them and they don't look at me or respond to our being here, as a ghost would with us walk-ing into a scenario like this.

We came out of the cell and the director had a big grin on his face. "Terrific! You hit it on the nose, Annette," he shouted. He continued on with great enthusiasm, "During the most famous attempted escape, called the 'Battle of Alcatraz,' this cell became a bloody murder scene. Inmate Paul Bernard Coy and Joseph Paul Cretzer and four other men planned a daring escape that, if successful, would launch them into history as the first to successfully escape from The Rock. The convicts captured nine unarmed

Annette begins to sense what's in the cell

guards and locked them into cells #404 and #403 which were later changed to C-102 and C-104."

"So let me tell you what happened in this exact cell," he said in a deep voice. "It is interesting that you and Loyd chose cell #403 to go into as this is the cell that Joseph Paul Cretzer took his .45 automatic revolver to and, leaning up against the bars of #403, began shooting rounds into the cramped cell of four guards and Officer Miller. Officer Miller was killed in cold blood and the others were all shot, injured, and left to die. They laid there for ten hours, with blood everywhere before the siege was over."

LOYD: As often happens in working with Annette, she picked up on a tragic scenario of history.

ANNETTE: The director wanted us to continue down the corridor of Seedy Street. Loyd and I started to walk down the long hallway when suddenly my legs began to shake and get very weak and I again broke out in goose bumps. I stopped and took a couple of deep breaths.

LOYD: *Are you alright, Annette?*

ANNETTE: I closed my eyes before responding with: *I can tell you one thing, my knees are shaking. My head is spinning and I feel a little faint.*

LOYD: *From back there, where we were in the cell?*

ANNETTE: *No, from something else! We are intruding on something. I am going to take a deep breath.*

Loyd quickly had his meter pointed out in front of me, waving it in the air to see if there was something that would register.

LOYD: I'd rarely seen Annette overcome by such a reaction. It was odd that I was not getting a thing when it was my experience, having done so many investigations with her, that I would tune into something when she had a big reaction. I thought perhaps she might be having a precognitive reaction, that we were about to encounter something, rather than something being with us at that moment.

ANNETTE: I was dizzy and felt short of breath and slowly looked to my left. There was a narrow walkway going from A Block toward a larger room that had shelves along the wall. Beige-painted steel bars lined the entrance and exit with the walls going up to the third level. Even though I felt strange, I still wanted to walk in there.

Loyd during the Alcatraz investigation

Loyd and David followed me in, but the camera crew didn't. Instead, they went toward the larger room that had been the library for the prison. As I walked in closer I began to hear voices.

[Whispering] *Loyd, can you hear that, can you hear them talking?*

LOYD: *No, I can't hear any voices. What do you hear?*

David also indicated he was hearing nothing. I placed the natural EMF device on the floor and turned it on, still using the standard meter as well.

ANNETTE: *There are all these men walking and shuffling in a line and they are whispering to one another. I am trying to hear what they are saying but can't make it out.*

LOYD: *Annette, what are you seeing now?*

Just then, both EMF sensors began registering higher magnetic fields, fluctuating wildly. I had to reset my standard TriField to be less sensitive so it could register on a larger scale (more energy).

As this was happening, I began to feel pressure in the front of my fore-head and face—my sinuses were shutting down a bit, as had happened in so many other cases, and was my first regular indication or patterning that led me to understand that I, too, was sensitive to psychic phenomena in the environment.

I have learned to "sense" things a bit differently in the last few years, maybe because part of my preparation currently involves taking a good decongestant before heading out on an investigation. Hate those sinus headaches, paranormally caused or not.

ANNETTE: *The guards were not in this hallway, but stood on either side of the gates of this passageway. Oh, my gosh, I could hear the men telling each other things about what was going on, fascinating! Whispering, pssst, psst, I hear talking, talking! They're not supposed to talk, Loyd, but I hear them whisper-ing in here! It's like the guards are not in here. Lots of men, bald headed, short haired, gosh, I think they lost their hair because the malnutrition was bad.*

I looked over at Loyd, who is a bit follicle-challenged himself, and he made a face at the bald comment. I began to giggle a bit. *I am sorry Loyd.*

[Note from Loyd: A park employee I met in May, 2010, who has exten-sive knowledge of the history and features of the prison, reviewed this chapter for me. He told me that many of the men shaved their heads, but there is no historical evidence of malnutrition.]

LOYD: I kept checking my EMF sensors and declared:

Yeah, I started to feel something in here too. The highest reading is right in the middle of the hallway.

*Annette holds her hands out in front of her to help her
sense any accessible energy*

ANNETTE: *I can hear footsteps, like this, shuffling.* [Mimics the foot-steps] *They are whispering all at the same time. This is definitely another incredible impression. Darn, thought we had really run into a ghost this time.*

I wanted to stay there and see if I could strain and hear more of the con-versations of the prisoners, but the director wanted us to go on and didn't seem to give a hoot about this incredible impression.

Loyd and I next walked into this open space with shelving on the walls, David followed.

The director said, "Do you pick up anything in here?

We walked around the room and all I could pick up was that a confron-tation and loud noises had taken place in there at some time. It felt heavy, but I didn't sense any impressions. The meters weren't picking up anything out of the ordinary either.

"Let's go this way," the director waved to us. We followed him through a floor-to-ceiling off-white metal cell doorway and I suddenly felt cold all over. Breathing became a problem as we inched our way towards a row of cells with solid metal doors.

The director told us that these were the isolation cells that they called "The Hole."

The solitary confinement cellblock

By this time I was shivering a bit, due to my nervous system, I am sure, not the cold in the air.

Loyd held my arm and wanted to make sure that I was alright. The director said, "I want you both to go into some of these isolation cells and tells us what you experience."

I remember gulping and thinking to myself, "I don't really want to go in there as I can already feel the darkness in this area of the prison."

Loyd looked at me and nodded, "Ok, let's go in."

We slowly entered Cell D-14. The air was freezing, almost like walking into an open freezer, and I immediately began having more problems breathing. I glanced at the thick steel door that stood open. Shivering, I called out to the director, "Don't close that door!"

LOYD: Again, my sinuses were acting up big time and I felt another pressure of sorts. A bit of nausea struck but passed quickly. All of this happened within a moment of Annette's reaction.

ANNETTE: It was a dark steel cell, no window, and with a hole in the center of the room, which must have been used as the toilet. I closed my eyes and tried to pick up what had happened in this horrible space and began to talk aloud: *Oh dear, this is not good! This is so sad. I am covered with goose bumps!*

Loyd leaned over to see my arms and witnessed the goose bumps covering the flesh.

My voice went up as I continued on: *There is a man, slight of build, pounding his forehead with his fists and shouting and screaming … Oh, my God, he begins to walk over to the wall and pounds his head against the cold steel. He is not talking with me and not paying any attention to us in here. This is a very powerful impression!*

LOYD: I was becoming a little concerned about Annette's reactions and said: *Annette, remember this is just a recording.*

I walked around the confined cell and pointed toward the center of the room. *We are getting a high reading here on the EMF meters.*

ANNETTE: My sense of smell became quite acute as I turned to Loyd, *I smell something dead! He died in here!*

LOYD: I'd placed the natural EMF meter on the floor, and held the other. The natural meter was beginning to fluctuate like crazy, registering some kind of real energy shift.

We are getting some natural EM fluctuation, possibly a geomagnetic field, putting out some real energy under the building.

ANNETTE: My feeling was that even though this was a psychic recording, I didn't care, just let me out of here! As I left the cell, I remarked to everyone that this was very interesting because normally when I am feeling the impressions, I don't get such a physical kind of tag. I could really feel this guy pounding his head on the wall.

LOYD: *That was some strong impression.*

ANNETTE: *Yes, such a different heaviness and almost like the end of the world for them! They couldn't see any new beginnings for themselves. That's the feeling I get in my body, it pervades this whole area here, it's just awful.*

LOYD: The sinus and other pressure was present for me the entire time I was in the cell. As I exited the cell, the sensations lifted almost immediately. A strong emotional impression, indeed.

ANNETTE: The director told us that there was an event in the 1940s of a prisoner being locked in 14D, screaming throughout the night that a creature with glowing eyes was killing him. The next day when the guards came to feed him they found the man strangled to death in the cell. It seems no one ever claimed responsibility for the convict's death. [Note from Loyd: On the other hand, despite what the director said, my current source of historical information has informed me that this was a rumor—there was a man who hanged himself in that cell (self-strangulation), but no real evidence of anyone who claimed there was a creature with glowing eyes.]

We continued on our tour down a hallway that let us into the commissary. To the left were the stairs to the hospital. There was a metal chain across the entrance that read, "DO NOT ENTER." Tours were not allowed up there, but arrangements had been made for us. I knew this was going to be exciting. We slowly climbed the stairs, anticipating that maybe we would finally see a ghost.

LOYD: While thus far I was excited by the number of residual impressions present in Alcatraz, I felt perhaps my pre-visit assessment was correct. No ghosts, just residual haunting.

ANNETTE: As we got upstairs, Loyd swung open the old heavy metal floor-to-ceiling barred doors. There was a squeaking sound, like this mammoth door hadn't been opened in a long time. It was truly like stepping into a horror movie with squeaking doors and big metal locks. The camera and sound man wanted to hear the sound of the keys turning the metal lock, so we got the full stereo sound of what it was like to hear what these unfortunate men experienced. My mind raced with pictures of pain and anguish that we would encounter next as we carefully stepped into the darkness of the second floor.

I was again having trouble breathing, and Loyd seemed to be having a reaction, as well.

LOYD: The pressure was building for me as we entered the area, though not like in The Hole. Annette asked if the EMF meter was registering anything. I looked down at the standard meter and told her that I was noting a much higher than baseline reading as we walked along.

ANNETTE: We inched our way down the long dark corridor and came upon the first door. I peered in and saw an operating table at the end of the second room. I instantly felt like I wanted to throw up.

I hadn't said anything, and Loyd looked in for a moment and quickly backed out of the doorway announcing, "Oh, I don't want to go in there! My sinuses are acting up very badly, I'm feeling nauseous—this is not a good sign for me." His face was ghostly white, with small beads of perspiration forming on his forehead. He said he felt dizzy.

I felt that atrocities had occurred in that operating room—I didn't want to enter it. Perhaps operations had been performed without a great deal of anesthesia, as I could hear men screaming and screaming, and that was enough for me.

Loyd told me later that the operating room reminded him of the same energy that he felt when he visited a prison down in Australia. He said it was horrible.

LOYD: In fact, I distinctly recall the same experience—especially the intense nausea and dizziness—in a chamber in the Darwin prison where they used to execute prisoners by hanging.

ANNETTE: Taking a deep breath, we continued down the hallway and went by several doors until we came to a cell door. I stopped before it.

I want to go in here. This is very heavy. Got the meters?

In the hospital area

LOYD: [Letting out a big sigh] *Yeah, I can feel it too. Are you sure you want to go in there?*

ANNETTE: *Oh, my knees are shaking and I have goose bumps everywhere. Loyd, we definitely need to go in here.*

LOYD: *You think so?*

ANNETTE: Stepping through the portal was like going into another world.

Oh, my! Woof! Oh, the walls are screaming. Like somebody was, oh gosh, sane one minute and insane the next moment.

The room was quite large in comparison to a regular cell—almost like a double cell, long and narrow with a window at the end. I was magnetized to the walls and began running my hands over and over the unkempt pale green institution stucco, pitted and broken. My voice began to rise as I was talking faster and faster. I began to see letters, cards, and pictures pinned up on these craggy walls, creating a colorful collage of a person's life. Books, books were everywhere, almost like a library against one wall. I was definitely in a video, an impression that was the strongest I had ever experienced.

Loyd's meters weren't picking up too much in this cell, and he kept walking out of the room, as if he didn't want to be in that psychotic energy; it made him too nervous.

LOYD: Unlike the other chamber down the hall, what I was feeling came in waves. The nausea and dizziness, as well as some weird sense of "noise" in my head like loud static, kept coming and going. This made it hard for me to stay in the cell for more than a minute at a time.

As far as the EMF meters were concerned, there was only a slight rise above the general low reading of most of the island and prison.

ANNETTE: I continued talking about all the things that were invading my mind. Then a sweeping feeling of a very sick mind came forward, a mind that was as calm and placid as a baby and then suddenly violent as a lion going for the kill. A thin man with large, dark, bulging eyes began to appear; his face had a hallow look, high cheek bones and kind of an angular jaw, and thinning hair. The eyes, they really stood out and I saw that he wore glasses. I wasn't sure if he wore them all the time. He looked like he hadn't eaten in days and was not being fed properly. [Note from Loyd: Our current source on the island states there was no malnutrition, but also stated that Stroud thought body hair was unclean and shaved himself completely, giving him the look of someone malnourished.]

I saw him reading and studying something, at times wearing glasses. As I watched this scene I began to see the personality as being very schizophrenic, definitely psychotic. He was isolated in his mind and didn't much pay attention to the outside world. I turned toward the wall on my left and saw the name Robert S. written there.

The director said, "Annette, this is the cell of the famous 'Birdman,' Robert Stroud. You have pegged it right on the money!"

Robert "The Bird Man" Stroud's cell

LOYD: Okay, yes, we knew Stroud had been a prisoner. But there was absolutely nothing at all to indicate that he'd been kept on this floor, let alone in this bigger-than-normal cell.

ANNETTE: They brought in a large photo of Robert Stroud and placed it in the middle of the cell. Stunned, I shouted out: *Oh, my God. Yes, that's him, that's what I saw. I just saw a little bit more hair on the top of his head.*

LOYD: *Certainly nothing like Burt Lancaster, who played him in the movie.*

Originally convicted of manslaughter, Robert Stroud, a.k.a. The Birdman of Alcatraz, was one of the most notable inmates ever to serve time there. Stroud spent seventeen years on Alcatraz, six years in segregation in D Block and eleven years in the prison hospital, and was never introduced into the general population. Like Al Capone, Stroud had enjoyed many privileges that were not allotted to fellow inmates at his previous residence, Leavenworth Federal Prison in Kansas.

Contrary to popular legend, The Birdman of Alcatraz was never permitted to keep any birds while on Alcatraz, enduring the deepest lock-down of his Alcatraz imprisonment in the hospital ward.

While at Leavenworth, he raised and sold canaries and wrote his famous book on bird disease, which led to Thomas E. Gaddis writing a book about Stroud called *Birdman of Alcatraz.*

But he was hardly the serene soul Burt Lancaster portrayed in the movie, as he was known to have a violent and unpredictable temper.

LOYD: If Annette—and I—were picking up on Stroud (and Annette's perceptions certainly indicated *she* was), it definitely was an impression, not Stroud's ghost. Stroud did not finish out his sentence in Alcatraz, nor did he die there. In 1959, he was transferred to the Medical Center for Federal Prisoners in Springfield, Missouri, where, on November 21, 1963, he was found dead from natural causes.

ANNETTE: We finished up the shoot with more camera shots of us walking down the hall and proceeded back to our original spot in Block A. After recap interviews about how we felt about our jaunt in Alcatraz and what we uncovered in our travels that night, we returned to Michigan Avenue and had an interview with ranger John Cantwell.

The ranger told us some stories known by the guards. Block C's utility corridor is said to be haunted by three prisoners who attempted escape and were killed there. We were not allowed in this area.

Cantwell described former prisoner Whitey Thompson, who told his story to visitors about a "silhouette" of a man on Michigan Avenue. He said the entity stood looking at him for a few minutes until Whitey ran toward him, which was when the silhouette disappeared.

Loyd uses a TriField Meter to determine EMF levels in a cell

Ranger Cantwell claimed that Broadway in particular gives off "an interesting vibe." Others who have worked as guards in the prison have told stories of inexplicable noises of cells slamming shut, screams, crashing noises, and foul smells inconsistent with the usual foul smells of a prison.

Needless to say, the director was thrilled at what we discovered and felt this was going to be a terrific segment in this show.

LOYD: All of what we experienced and were told by the ranger supports the notion that Alcatraz has much in the way of diverse residual psychic impressions. The good news is that such things can be experienced by a wide range of visitors, and because they are impressions they can't interact with us. On the other hand, because of the negative nature of so many of the impressions, people can most certainly feel them as being "bad," as Annette and I did.

One other note: The segment did indeed turn out to be quite interesting, and, as of this writing, can be found on YouTube. Just search for "Annette Martin" and "Alcatraz" and you'll happen upon it. That was the only time I've been to Alcatraz so far. But Annette did go back and did find a ghost....

Finding a Ghost at Alcatraz

ANNETTE: Several years went by and my husband and I were invited to take a special tour of Alcatraz by Jason Alexander and his wife Felicia Fowler-Alexander.

Felicia explained, "I worked in the cell house and supervised the evening tour, which was the big tour of the facility. I also worked in the bookstore when they needed help. It was a really fun job. Jason worked in the administration department, but he also worked on the docks and greeted the boats as they came in because he has such a big voice."

They wanted to show us places that the tours are not allowed to go. How exciting I thought—maybe I will really run into a ghost this time.

We arrived on the Blue and Gold Fleet ferry in the late morning; it was cold and foggy, a typical San Francisco morning. Fortunately, we had bundled up well with long pants and ski jackets to keep out the wind. My husband Bruce had his camera and video camera in hand, just in case we ran into something interesting.

On our arrival, we began our tour down on the lower north side of the island by following a narrow, steep path that first led us to the guards' Bachelor Quarters, and just below that to another area.

I began to immediately pick up on young men—mostly Native American men. They were scared to death, and I heard them begin to chant as they sat in a circle on the dirt floor. They felt innocent, and the feeling was that they had been brought here because they were Native Americans. Some had feathers and they would do a feather ceremony asking the Great Spirit to help them.

I saw the guards peering through a big door at them as they were clapping their hands (because they had no drums).

Jason interrupted me at this point and acknowledged all that I had revealed. He said that it was quite common for them to bring the Native American young men here. It is said that the first death to occur on Alcatraz was that of a young male Native American trying to escape.

LOYD: Discussing this with Annette after her visit, it was clear that the residual hauntings were not restricted to just the prison area on Alcatraz.

ANNETTE: As we continued along the path, Jason pointed out that above us was the Officers' Club, and there on the rocks below was where the guards had found pieces of Frank Morris's clothing. Morris was one of the infamous trio (along with Clarence Anglin and his brother John) who disappeared from Alcatraz on June 11, 1962, in an incident that was the basis of the Clint Eastwood film *Escape from Alcatraz*. They were never seen or heard from again, and it's still assumed they drowned in the Bay.

We continued our walk and went through the powerhouse and made a stop at the Industries Building. This is the building where the convicts washed, dried, ironed and folded the laundry. I was quite surprised when Jason told us that they did the laundry for the Navy!

It is a huge building that goes on forever. We walked through the first room that housed the washers and dryers and I began to intuitively see the long tables they used for folding. The equipment had been left there, rusting and deteriorating from lack of care. The ceiling must have been at least sixteen feet high. Solid concrete walls ran along the eastern side of this large building. There were walls made of glass separating areas of this room. Thin metal lines in the glass and holes dotting it created a unique batik painting on each pane.

Jason said that the holes in all the windows had been done by the Native Americans that occupied Alcatraz after it had been closed. It felt like they had used it for target practice.

"There is a lot of energy in here, really bad guys. This is definitely an impression and I am covered in goose bumps. I am picking up a big, well-known tough guy, with a great deal of anger. He must have had words with the guards as I hear a bit of a scuffle," I told them.

Jason smiled and said, "Yes, Al Capone worked in here doing laundry before he became too ill to work."

We went into the next room, which was far more comfortable, dry, and toasty warm. Along the whole western wall were windows, again with tiny metal strands running through each pane. But the view out these windows as the sun shone through was spectacular. I walked hurriedly over to them and gasped at the site of the Golden Gate Bridge in all its glory. You look straight on at the golden beauty as it sits in the gateway to San Francisco. I could just imagine what a beautiful sunset looks like from this vantage point.

Jason told us that this room was where the convicts of Alcatraz made pants for the Army and gloves for the Navy. A very industrious room for sure.

I had a nice warm feeling inside and was wondering what I was picking up. Bruce, Jason, and Felicia were walking around talking. Something made me stop, take a deep breath and close my eyes for a moment. The goose bumps began to come out on my arms and face as I opened my eyes to see something misty and moving.

"Oh, guess what guys," I gasped. "I think we have a ghost that walks through here. He is slight of build, maybe late twenties or early thirties."

Jason and Felicia stopped in their tracks and Bruce came over to me with his camera. I began to talk out loud to the young man that no one else could see or hear. I asked him who he was.

"Allen, Allen is my name," he told me.

It was quiet for a few moments and I asked him to tell me about himself.

"I was in another prison before. Was rowdy, they said I was a difficult prisoner. They called me a troublemaker," the apparition said.

Knowing now that he could communicate quite well, I continued asking questions."Why are you here in this room," I asked out loud.

There was silence for a moment and then he replied back, "Nowhere to go. I was put in prison for making money, counterfeiting, and I also killed someone in self-defense."

Jason shook his head in agreement and remarked, "Yes, that is how a lot of them got here."

Allen continued to talk to me, "I was an alcoholic and had anger with anyone with authority."

I broached the question of how he died here at Alcatraz.

The voice became a little more agitated at this point and he said, "They let me die, I was sick, my stomach, terrible pains."

The room where Annette encounterd the ghost of Jack Allen

Continuing to speak out loud, I said, "I am terribly sorry, Allen, that they did not take good care of you. But I can help you go into the light and join your family. Would you like to do that?"

He replied, slowly and softly, "I am Catholic and because of all the bad things that I have done, I am afraid. It's warm and quiet here in this room, so I stay here."

There was silence for a few moments; everyone stood waiting for his reply. He finally said to me, "I don't want to leave!"

Jason spoke out loud and said, "Yes, people just don't come down here. So it is quiet all the time."

It has been my practice to never force a ghost to go into the Light. He seemed to be quite content here in the empty, warm room, so I didn't proceed any further in getting him upset and angry. I thanked Allen for communicating with me and perhaps I will come back another day to talk with him.

Felicia interrupted at this point and said, "There is a book with all the names of the people who died here at Alcatraz. I will get you that book, Annette."

Alcatraz Island, from San Francisco Bay (pachd.com)

"Yes, he doesn't want to cause any more trouble, he is just here," I concluded. At this point we left the building.

We made a beeline for the bookstore to see what we could find and, lo and behold, there on page 94 of Michael Esslinger's book *Alcatraz: A Definitive History of the Penitentiary Years*, was "Jack W. Allen."

According to the book, prisoner number 211, Jack W. Allen, incarcerated for counterfeiting, had required gastric ulcer surgery early in the year. Not long after he died from pneumonia on January 17, 1936.

Rumors spread that the prison medical technician had, through negligence, permitted Allen to die. Allen had been put into solitary confinement for long periods of time, even though he complained of being in pain.

We found our ghost of Alcatraz!

LOYD: This is a really impressive bit of spirit communication, especially with the factual back-up to what she'd received in talking with the ghost. I really wish I'd been able to participate in this visit with Annette. We'll have to make arrangements to return and speak with Allen and see if we can help him in some other way.

The Moss Beach Distillery Restaurant

140 Beach Way, Moss Beach, CA 94038

This lonely restaurant sits on the hill above a Northern California beach. From time to time, fog and mists swirl around it and the homes that are on either side. Tourists and locals alike come for the excellent food and the magnificent Pacific Ocean view. And some come for the ghost.

For the Moss Beach Distillery is never empty as long as the spirit called "the Blue Lady" roams its interior and the beach below … the beach where she was murdered.

The plaque in front of the Distillery

Patrons are not the only ones attracted to the place and its ghost: the Distillery and the Blue Lady have been featured on numerous national and local TV shows, including *Unsolved Mysteries, Sightings*, A&E's *They See Dead People, America's Most Haunted Places*, and numerous other shows on the History Channel, the Discovery Channel, the Travel Channel, TechTV (now G4) and more.

The restaurant known today as the Moss Beach Distillery was originally built as a house, but when it was taken over in 1926 by restaurateur Frank Torres, it became known as Frank's Roadhouse. The establishment also included a small hotel for special guests.

During Prohibition, with the beach below a smuggling point for liquor, the restaurant was a "protected" speakeasy where anyone who was anyone could still drink to his heart's content. The place was incredibly popular with the locals, politicos, and celebrities from the growing film industry.

The beach where the Blue Lady was found … dead

While there have been three possible deaths connected to the identity of the Blue Lady, only one seems to fit the time frame of the first sightings, as well as the perceptions of a variety of psychics who have visited the place since 1990. The other deaths were much more mundane. While it may be the ghost herself who's promoting the more romanticized tale, it does seem to fit according to locals and historians.

During the early 1930s, a piano player at the restaurant was graced with the presence of a beautiful young woman night after night. It is said that the two had an ongoing affair.

Unfortunately, the young woman, who is said to have worked in the hotel that once stood where the parking lot is now, was married—though supposedly separated from a husband, who mistreated her. She was most often seen wearing bright blue clothing, and was given the nickname "the Blue Lady" even before her death.

One night her husband showed up in the bar. A fight ensued between the two men, which eventually moved outside the place, and supposedly onto the beach. Just what happened is not recorded anywhere, but the beautiful young woman, dressed that evening in a long blue dress, was found the next morning on the beach. She had been stabbed to death—the piano player (who may have had family ties to the owner, Frank Torres) was apparently bruised, but alive. Of the husband, there was never again any sign.

The woman in blue was dead, her husband gone, her lover still tickling the ivories night after night. It was your basic lover's tragedy, ripe for a haunting. And of course, that's exactly what happened as within days people began sighting an apparition of a lady in a blue dress, first on the beach, then eventually in the restaurant and hotel.

For decades since the early 1930s, the sightings continued in and around the restaurant, with folks regularly seeing the Blue Lady in spots such as the ladies room, the bluff outside the restaurant, the patio, and more.

In the 1970s, with new owners actually living in the place (there was a living area where the office now sits downstairs from the dining rooms), the visual sightings tapered off a bit, but apparently the ghost learned how to move things such as lamps, bottles, and glassware. Even chairs reportedly moved of their own accord. And, as visual sightings dropped, people began reporting intense subjective feelings of a presence.

In one particular spot in the main dining area, patrons would regularly ask employees about the table where they were sitting, as they felt a presence or something strange; and people who were unfamiliar with the legend of the place routinely have asked if the restaurant is haunted.

Since the 1970s, some of reported phenomena, besides actual sightings of the apparition, include:

- Boxes of liquor stacked against the only door into a room—from the inside.
- The outer door of the Fitzgerald Room opened again and again on request of a medium from Japan.
- The end lamps at the bar and the lamp over the hostess station swing of their own accord.
- A chair levitated and flipped over in front of three people.
- Lights turn on and off by themselves.
- Flying—but not breaking—glassware.
- During a major renovation for earthquake safety, workers reported unexplained happenings with the plumbing and lights.
- Male workers in the kitchen reported being pinched or whacked on the rear end when bent over.
- For a time, the phone lines would all ring at once, though no one would be on the other end and the phone company said there was no record of anyone calling.
- During a TV shoot, all the chairs on the patio toppled over like dominoes in front of the producer and host.

• Just before an October 2009 live radio broadcast from the restaurant, in which Annette and Loyd participated, a dining room chair was seen by three people to fall over on its own.

LOYD: I'm going to present this story from my perspective, as we thought it would give you a good feel for the non-psychic guy's perceptions and conclusions. In some respects, this is both an easy and tough place to write about, because we have *so* much information, so many sessions recorded with Annette and the ghost, and so many witnesses. One of these days, Annette and I will do an entire book on just this restaurant and its wonderful ghost, who we've come to call Cayte.

But in the meantime, for an extensive discussion of my own history with the restaurant, see my book *A Paranormal Casebook: Ghost Hunting in the New Millennium* (Atriad Press, 2005).

In some respects, this has to be my favorite haunted place, and I end up there several times a year—though admittedly mostly because of the exceptional food and view. But I always have to put the word out that I'm headed there in hopes that Cayte will be present to hang out with me. I do this mentally and by letting Annette and a couple of other psychics who have been in touch with the Blue Lady know so they can also send out that mental alert.

I've been involved with the Distillery longer than Annette, but she is certainly the psychic with the most experience with the ghost.

I began my in-depth investigations of the Distillery in 1991 for Japanese TV, accompanied by a team of folks who were part of my Office of Paranormal Investigations. The Tokyo Broadcasting production team brought along famed Japanese medium Aiko Gibo.

Mrs. Gibo quickly identified a woman in a blue dress as the resident spirit.

Well known today for its ghost of a woman who was killed as a result of a lovers' triangle, in 1991 the Distillery's "Blue Lady" was only a local legend with next to no media attention having been paid to its haunting.

Aiko Gibo spent time in communication with the Blue Lady. She seemed to unfocus her attention for a moment and immediately began conversing with the spirit. One very interesting feature of her communication was that her end of the conversation was held in Japanese. She explained to us that her actual communication with the ghost was of a telepathic nature. Her verbalizing was for the benefit of the TV cameras—and for our benefit a translator gave a running commentary of what was being said.

The main/original dining room

Mrs. Gibo provided several bits of information about the apparition, and what she said fit what we subsequently learned from a local historian and several long-time local residents, as well as from other psychics I've worked with over the years.

That other stories have floated around as to who the Blue Lady was is likely a result of a general lack of death records from the specific area during the Prohibition Era, making it tough to pin down her actual identity. Any woman who verifiably died tragically anywhere near the location—even before it was built—became a possible name behind the apparition, even if she had no connection to the building or the plot of land.

However, the story we have comes from numerous and diverse sources, such as local historians, local residents, normal folks and psychics alike who have had "conversations" with the ghost. In other words, the story of the Blue Lady comes to us from both the living and the dead, even if the actual records don't exist.

While most TV shows and books covering the Distillery report the love triangle, the most common alternate story is of a woman who died in a car accident a little way down the road from the restaurant. That there have been sightings of a ghost at the site of the accident supports the existence of *that* particular entity.

"Cayte's table" in the main dining room, where the piano stood during Prohibition

However, research on the car accident story shows that there are a couple of problems in connecting it with the Moss Beach Distillery. First of all, the accident happened in 1919, several years *before* the building was constructed (1926), so the woman who died would have had absolutely no connection to the original home which became Frank's Place. Secondly, the apparition seen on the road was a woman in white, not a woman wearing blue. So, it's the right general vicinity, but not the right ghost.

Mrs. Gibo, in conversation with the Blue Lady, picked up other elements, including the names "Elizabeth," "Claire," and "Kate," which have been perceived by other psychics and witnesses. Mrs. Gibo connected all three names to the Blue Lady, and one other psychic, Kathy Reardon, also picked up that the ghost's first name was Elizabeth and her middle name was Claire, although she picked up nothing about "Kate." That was a minor mystery not solved until Annette Martin came into the picture, and we learned later the spelling was odd as well: "Cayte."

The back door in the Fitzgerald Room that opened on its own

Mrs. Gibo and the ghost, both seated at a table in the main dining room—well, we could see Mrs. Gibo at least—seemed to share a joke or two, as the medium was observed laughing from time to time. Just before the first communication session ended, Mrs. Gibo reached into her bag and pulled out an American fashion magazine, flipping through it and pointing to various models wearing different dresses. It's interesting to note that the Blue Lady, who had previously been seen only wearing blue dresses, has subsequently been sighted wearing more fashionable black cocktail and evening dresses and other modern fashions.

Later, while in a then-unfinished addition to the restaurant destined to become a second dining room, the medium described the spirit moving to a back door. She told us the ghost would open the door for us. This was followed by the door—a push bar on the inside and only a keyhole on the outside—actually opening. I placed one of my team outside that door, and we all watched in amazement as this was repeated several times, each time with the medium describing the apparition's location and actions accompanying the door movement.

When I next saw Mrs. Gibo two days later, she remarked that the Blue Lady had come to her hotel room in San Francisco for a visit and follow-up conversation to what they'd talked about at the restaurant. Apparently, the ghost needed further advice on fashion.

I continued to work with Mrs. Gibo on a number of television shows, looking at haunted locations in several places in the U.S. and overseas, but she never made it back to the Distillery.

Kathy Reardon, who had worked with me on a number of cases before moving to the East Coast, was the second psychic I took to the Distillery in the early 1990s. As with Mrs. Gibo, the information about the Blue Lady's death, the names "Elizabeth," "Claire," and "Cayte," and a reason she was still present came through. Interestingly, Reardon told us some of the ghost's recollections of her interactions with past owners and employees, experiences that were confirmed through our interview process. Additionally, Reardon noted the Blue Lady's sense of humor about her situation and interactions, and the ghost's very light-hearted feeling of approval that we were working to understand her situation. This is something that has come through from every psychic practitioner who has communicated with the entity since then.

In the mid 1990s, I began my collaboration with Annette. It was in 1997 that Annette and I joined forces on the Distillery, a team which continues to this day—our last visit together was October 29, 2009.

Besides our investigative visits, we did several séance-type communication sessions there for the first few years. It seemed that from the very first time we visited the restaurant together, Annette and the Blue Lady hit it off. The names "Elizabeth Claire" and "Cayte" continued to come through, and Annette felt the name Cayte was some kind of nickname for her.

Numerous other tidbits of information would come through Annette that I ended up confirming either against what the historians could tell me, my records of what other psychics had said, or through some of the local residents and witnesses.

Let me make a few observations about what one sees when Annette is doing her thing at the Distillery. It's been interesting to observe that when Annette cannot sense the Blue Lady, neither can others. It is clear to me that this is not simply a case of one psychic following the lead of another, as the others are typically unaware of Annette's assessment of the ghost's absence.

In the majority of visits where the Blue Lady is present, Annette typically feels her presence before seeing or hearing her. She first reports the goose bumps on her arms as in other cases, a reaction which can be observed by others. She will report feeling the Blue Lady's emotions, then feeling her presence before beginning a communication process. She

On the patio

reports sometimes perceiving the apparition in a visual or auditory mode, but this is always preceded by a kinesthetic sense of the presence. She is able to identify the specific location of the apparition, and we have been able to find correspondence between Annette's location of the ghost with strong, and sometimes oscillating, readings on a magnetometer, as well as with other signs of anomalies detected by different technology.

While in a fairly normal state, Annette will sometimes converse aloud, sometimes silently, with the apparition. I am able to ask questions of Cayte, which Annette has said the ghost sometimes hears directly, but sometimes must be repeated by Annette either mentally or aloud.

Annette will sometimes shift to a less normal state by closing her eyes and focusing on the communication process. There doesn't seem to be any particular difference in the quality of the conversation in this mode, but Annette seems to be able to pick up more of the spirit's emotional state and reactions.

Annette seems to need to be where the ghost is to communicate with it and that can be just about anywhere in the restaurant. However, I have noticed that on most daytime visits, the best communication with the ghost appears to occur outside on the patio overlooking the beach where she was murdered.

In our sessions with the spirit (some would call these "séances"), which can take place in either the original or newer dining room, we set a maximum time for the sessions, though sometimes we do not reach that time before either Annette or the Blue Lady plead exhaustion. Sessions have been generally between thirty and sixty minutes in length.

Annette sits quietly, takes several deep breaths, and appears to go into a relaxed state. After two minutes or so she begins speaking aloud to Cayte and almost immediately states that she's getting a response. During the session, Annette begins by passing along questions from the sitters to the ghost, and eventually switches randomly between a third person and first person voice with her answers, seemingly going into a deeper state of relaxation. It seems that for some questions, but not for others, the spirit is speaking directly through Annette. There is a sense of effort for the responses provided in first person and much less effort for those passed along in third person.

In the communication sessions with Cayte, Annette has stated and demonstrated (and, outwardly, Annette has portrayed Cayte's distress) that the ghost becomes upset whenever her husband—her murderer—is mentioned. Very interestingly, during the emotional distress displayed when the subject of her husband comes up, the two magnetic field detectors I typically have beside Annette, which each measure different frequency ranges, tend to register high readings.

In these sessions, we've asked Cayte a number of questions about her history, the history of the restaurant, and her existence as a ghost.

Why was she still there haunting the restaurant? Apparently, she had such fond memories of the place when she was alive—mainly, we assume, because the love of her life was working there—that it was the logical place for her to stay while waiting for her lover to die and for his spirit to find her. The Blue Lady has also passed along her opinion that the more fun people have at the restaurant, the more fun she has as well in her "afterlife."

In 1999, I was able to spend two good chunks of time at the Distillery for an investigation and multiple communication sessions. On a Friday and Saturday night, starting before and lasting well after closing, I had a team of folks throughout the restaurant. Naturally Annette was key to the event and took the lead, but because of the size of the place and the team, I had a couple of other volunteer psychics with us: Stache Margaret Murray, who joined us for the first time, and Pamela Heath, a parapsychologist colleague with psychic abilities, who was part of the Office of Paranormal Investigations team for some time.

The first night we had a séance also attended by a few members of the press. During that session, several interesting things came up in our questioning of the ghost.

Through Annette, we got some interesting responses to the question of her identity, name, and even nickname. She identified herself as Elizabeth Claire Donovan, from Indiana. She and her husband came to San Francisco to make a new life for themselves, but she'd only been married to him a short time. She soon discovered he had a violent temper and would beat her. She left him, essentially escaping down the coast to Half Moon Bay, the town just south of Moss Beach. She ended up getting a job at the Marine View Hotel next to Frank's Roadhouse. She met the piano player and fell in love. We knew the rest.

At the time, we didn't know that the last name she gave, Donovan, was not actually her own married name. That came much later.

I asked her where the name "Kate" came from. Through Annette, she replied that she'd always liked that name, but not the spelling. So she decided to spell the name as Cayte.

I asked why she actually adopted that name. Annette laughed and said "She says she's dead, and can be called anything she wants, right?" We all laughed too.

"But why that spelling?" I asked.

"She says that if you can spell your name with one 'L,' she can spell her name C-A-Y-T-E," said Annette through some more hearty laughter. Pretty much everyone there got the joke, and the mood lightened even more than before. Our sessions with Cayte are almost always light-hearted and giggly.

That same session, we had a very interesting tidbit of information come out that we initially thought would be unverifiable, but it turned out that another case that I was involved in would later provide the key.

I began to ask questions in a different vein, specifically if she could recall some of the events that went on at Frank's Roadhouse while she was alive. As we'd heard about a history of booze smuggling during Prohibition, I wanted to know if one other piece we'd gotten from the historian—that Frank's Place was protected—conformed to Cayte's recollection.

"Cayte, were there any raids on Frank's Place when it was a speakeasy?" I asked.

Annette related to us that Cayte was firm that the place itself had not been raided, but that the beach below had been the site of several arrests and three major raids. Annette began to describe the raids, with G-men, local police, and of course the smugglers involved. Gunshots and deaths happened, she said. As this was going to be very difficult if not impossible to find records for, we put the information aside. All very *Untouchables*.

After the séance, on the second night, something very new and different happened to me, with Cayte.

But first, let me relate how the story of the three raids was confirmed, sort of.

Months after that weekend investigation at the Distillery, Stache Murray invited me and a couple of other investigators onto the *USS Hornet* Aircraft Carrier Museum, a decommissioned WWII aircraft carrier that sits in the water at Alameda near San Francisco. During our interviews about hauntings at the *Hornet* over the next couple of months, one of the witnesses related a tale of his own sighting of the Blue Lady during the 1950s, when he was twelve years old, and proceeded to provide support of the tale of the raids on the beach.

This witness, an ex-US Naval officer named Alan McKean, gave us some interesting facts about the early days of the Distillery. According to Alan, his father was an attorney for the State of California during Prohibition. He was asked to come along on three major raids aimed at the smugglers using the beach below the restaurant. The basic description of those raids, while described to Alan when he was much younger, matched what Cayte had told Annette. Corroboration, from a surprise source indeed!

So, what happened to me that second night?

After closing, we were spread throughout the restaurant, both to get baseline readings and psychic reads on the place, and to see where and when Cayte might make herself known to one or more of us.

I was alone in the bar area. I was taking magnetic readings behind the bar well after two in the morning when my magnetometer spiked quite high. At first, I thought I was picking up the ice machine or some other powered piece of equipment behind the bar. But there was no apparent source for the reading based on where I was standing.

Then, a moment later, I felt a tingling sensation on the back part of my body, followed by sort of a rippling effect. The tingling sensation passed completely through my body, stopped, then returned from the other direction. There was a pause, and it repeated. And repeated again.

I began timing the experience.

As the experience continued, I knew that somehow Cayte was getting my attention by moving through my body. I even got a mind's-eye perception of a very attractive woman in her twenties wearing a black dress, earrings, a pendant, and bracelets, in black heels, walking back and forth through me, giggling.

The bar area

After several passes and about two minutes of this, Annette, Pam, and Stache entered the room and stopped, staring at me. Annette began laughing, and one of them (I'm afraid I was too busy paying attention to the ghost) said, "Hey, she's walking right through you"—followed by more laughter from all three. Someone then said, "I think we scared her off," and indeed the tingling sensation ceased. In fact, it felt like the energy was moving off in the direction they indicated, and the magnetic reading dropped to baseline.

I asked them to each, separately, describe what the Blue Lady had been wearing (clothing, jewelry), how her hair was done, and even what she was doing. Their descriptions not only agreed with each other's, but also with that mental image I'd received, even the giggling.

What did it feel like? In general, the energy of the experience rocked my body a bit, somewhat like what one feels standing in ocean surf as the waves come in and out. The tingling sensation was a very light, positive feeling, probably because of what the ghost's intentions were—Annette says she was "trying to give you a thrill."

How did it really feel?

It felt good. (Don't tell my wife!)

Artist's conception of Cayte walking into Loyd

This was an exciting experience on so many levels for me, as it was certainly the closest encounter I'd ever had with an apparition. But it seemed to have a lasting effect, as ever since then I have noticed a particular sensation in myself whenever Annette or others think Cayte is around. It's very consistent.

The experience is now a bit of a joke between Annette and me. In interviews and events we do together, people sometimes kiddingly ask the question, "Can you have sex with a ghost?"

Annette immediately responds with "Loyd almost did." And, with a big laugh, "We don't know what might have happened if the others and I had

The Fitzgerald Room

not come into the room when we did. Cayte really likes Loyd."This always brings on more laughter and maybe a little blushing on my part.

Over the ten years since that experience, we've done numerous séances and other communication sessions with Cayte. As part of our following discussions with her, we focused on whether she knew it was unlikely her piano player boyfriend would actually be coming back for her.

Annette's connection with the ghost provided us with a hesitant yes, that she did understand that, but that she really still loved being there. Annette made it clear to her that this was all right, but that she could also move on when she wanted.

"I know, but I love it here," said Cayte through Annette.

According to Annette, "She's happy, she's flirtatious, and has no intention of leaving for good. She is so content because she's surrounded by people who are eating wonderful food and enjoying themselves immensely."

Annette and I asked her if she'd thought of traveling, besides visiting her (Annette) in San Jose, something Annette had related to us all earlier that evening. I had already mentioned that Cayte had visited with Mrs. Gibo in San Francisco after that initial investigation years before. But we suggested traveling farther away than San Francisco or San Jose. With more than a little humor, I told her, "You can go anywhere in the world you want. You're a ghost—you don't even have to pay for a plane ticket, it's all free!"

The response through Annette was quite positive, and Annette reinforced the idea. Little did I know that Cayte would take it to heart—or whatever passes for that with a floating consciousness. More on that in a moment.

At that same séance, a participant asked if Cayte had ever encountered any other ghosts. Apparently she had, both at the Distillery and nearby. We were told that other ghosts did occasionally stop by, some who had died long before and others more recently.

On a subsequent occasion, a new question was asked by a participant: "What did she miss most about being alive?"

"Sex and food," was the response through Annette, with a laugh.

I sidestepped the sex issue (having had that earlier "close encounter"): "Any particular food?"

"Strawberry ice cream, but really food in general," was the response.

"Cayte, I have some ideas as to how we can help with that. Let me work on it," I said.

Annette provided Cayte's reply as a real exclamation of excitement.

Let me stick with the food thing for a bit, and then I'll get back to Cayte's travels and our experiences with her.

Ankhasha Amenti, currently in the Seattle area, is another psychic I've worked with in the last few years, and who has also been present with Annette at the Distillery.

On her first visit to the Moss Beach Distillery, with Annette Martin and another psychic, Ankhasha perceived the Blue Lady in the same location and movements as Annette. Her description of the ghost's emotional state and general sense of being was extremely similar to what Annette perceived, though the two of psychics were not in each other's presence when the statements were made.

The Patio area that Annette has identified as Cayte's "entry" point

In September 2004, Ankhasha was visiting the Bay Area for a confer-ence dealing with training people to do remote viewing, and we decided to pay Cayte a visit—and have a nice lunch. As I mentioned, I've learned that I get a particular sensation when the Blue Lady's around. As soon as we walked downstairs, I felt that sensation. Without any prompting from me, Ankhasha immediately said, "Hi, Cayte," and led us outside on the patio overlooking the ocean. Ankhasha then got a faraway look in her eye, and let Cayte speak through her.

For about fifteen minutes, I had yet another conversation with the Blue Lady, but this time discussing some of the results of the last séance held with Annette. The communication centered on two topics: the ghost's per-ceptions of her existence and her interactions within the context of my investigations. The responses were similar to those provided by Annette in her communication sessions with Cayte, though I'd not discussed them with Ankhasha at all.

Based on the model that apparitions are communicating with us liv-ing folks telepathically, I again suggested to Cayte that there was a way in which she could taste food again, if Ankhasha—or anyone else—was especially willing.

Ghosts have no physical ears to hear with or eyes to see with. They receive perceptual information on a psychic level. I posited, why not taste-related sensations? I suggested that she focus on the sense and perceptions of taste (since the tongue tastes, but the mind perceives the tastes) of someone else. Ankhasha agreed to be that someone, and our lunch to be that meal.

As Cayte said good-bye, Ankhasha began to come out of her quite-altered state. Once fully recovered, I learned that this was something she'd experienced only on rare occasion, and that she could only remember little pieces of the conversation. She said that when this happens it doesn't feel like she is fully present, that it is more like she is stepping out of her body. She also said that "Cayte is going to do something special for you today."

We ended the brief session and went up to lunch. As we were eating, I noted that Ankhasha was beginning to seem a bit unfocused and distant. She nodded and almost immediately laughed aloud. This was followed by several bites of food. There was another laugh, and then she began to cry. Ankhasha began to describe how Cayte was tasting the food through her. For the rest of the meal, Ankhasha was picking up Cayte's emotional reactions, vacillating from sheer laughing to almost crying with happiness at the new discovery. The emotions coming from the entity were joyful, generating both laughter and tears of happiness, albeit via Ankhasha. I joked that maybe I ought to open a school for perception-deprived ghosts.

"It was like her soul touched mine for a moment and thanked me for allowing her to come in to my body and use it for that experience," said Ankhasha.

After lunch, Ankhasha and I went back downstairs and sat to discuss what had just happened. We were totally alone in the area just inside the patio. As I was asking her about how Cayte was reacting, I heard my first name called by a lyrical female voice, about three to four feet off to my left. No one was there or within earshot of us—and Ankhasha, who is not a ventriloquist, was speaking at the same time. Ankhasha asked, "Did she say something to you, Loyd?" She could hear the female voice, but could not make out what was said.

I was recording that conversation with Ankhasha, but there was no other voice on the recording.

I felt even more connected to Cayte than ever, having now heard her call out to me, something that has been reported by numerous employees over the years. Cayte had provided me with my first auditory experience of something paranormal, the something special she promised.

By the way, during the remote viewing conference, not only did I feel Cayte's presence while I was discussing the Distillery case, but Ankhasha and the also-present Pamela Heath saw her.

Now, back to the traveling ghost ….

A view of the inside patio downstairs

After Annette and I gave her some travel advice, apparently Cayte decided traveling was a very good idea. A few months later, I got an e-mail out of the blue from a woman claiming to be a medium in Paris, France. She said that a "spirit from your country" visited her, and she described a woman who sounded an awful lot like Cayte (based on the descriptions from Annette and other witnesses). She named her "Kate" and said the "spirit insisted I find you and tell you she was traveling and seeing the world." While not given my full name, the medium was apparently given enough information to find me on the Web.

On another occasion, when I was in Texas for a lecture, a woman approached me before the lecture, introduced herself as a local medium who knew a couple of my colleagues, and proceeded to tell me that "some ghost named Cayte" appeared to her the night before and helped her decide to attend my lecture, then asked her to apologize for her. Cayte had other places to visit and couldn't make my lecture.

A bit later, in 2005, I presented at a Parapsychology Foundation conference in Charlottesville, Virginia. During the presentation, when I spoke of Annette, the Distillery, and Cayte, I felt her presence. Ankhasha was in the audience, and I could see her smile and point to my left, where I had the sense of presence. When I finished, Ankhasha told me Cayte was present.

Perhaps more telling, three mediums in the audience came up separately and said they thought they saw a young woman standing to my left during the presentation.

Pamela Heath has said Cayte has visited her at her home in Alameda several times, and a non-professional medium in Canada has gotten in touch with me and reported many conversations with Cayte. Some of these conversations have been timed to coincide with comments from others who have independently mentioned Cayte discussing her visits to Pam and the Canadian medium.

Just as I have been to the restaurant without Annette, so too has she gone without me. Let me turn this over to her for an interesting story.

ANNETTE: A popular radio station in San Francisco, California, called and asked if I would do a séance during a special dinner party for a talk show hostess to be held at the Moss Beach Distillery. The arrangements were made and on Saturday, September 6, 1999, I arrived at the Distillery. We were given the newly redecorated Fitzgerald room facing the ocean. Dinner was delicious. Fifteen of us sat at a long table with me at the head of the table. As the dessert was being served, the manager of the station sitting next to the talk show hostess at the other end of the table asked if I would start the séance. I stood up for a moment to introduce myself to the party but as I sat back down I noticed a shadow that kept moving around behind the talk show hostess. Looking harder, I realized that this was Cayte—she became more visible as the seconds went on.

I explained that Cayte was indeed already in the room and that I was going to close my eyes for a moment and talk to her. I told the others to not be afraid to speak up if they had questions.

I closed my eyes, started to take my three deep breaths, but something jerked my eyes wide open. I looked down at the other end of the table and saw Cayte, clear as day standing behind the talk hostess and looking strangely at her hair. As I always do, I began to speak out loud to let them know what I was seeing and experiencing.

"Cayte, what are you looking at?" I asked.

No sooner had the words fallen out of my mouth when Cayte reached over to touch the hostess's long dark brown hair. Before I could say anything, I began to see pieces of her hair going up in the air. At this point, the woman screamed, "Oh, my God, she is touching my hair! Tell her to stop touching my hair!"

Everyone at the table was frozen in place and the manager was white as a sheet as he stared at long brown hair floating in the air.

Immediately I asked, "Cayte, what are you doing?"

Cayte responded, "I have never seen anything like this before," as she continued to lift another section of hair.

"Cayte, what are you talking about?" I asked, not having a clue as to why she was so preoccupied with the woman's hair.

"This is very strange," Cayte continued.

By this time the hostess was hysterical, crying, hyperventilating and trying to pull her hair down from floating in the air. I said in a firm voice, "Cayte, you are frightening her, you have to stop this!"

At that point the hair went down and Cayte moved closer to me. Trying to calm down the group, I asked if anyone had a question for Cayte. For the next half hour, our ghost answered mundane questions and finally made a move toward the woman at the other end of the table again.

Cayte again lifted a smaller section of hair as everyone gasped and the woman screamed, "Make her stop, make her stop!"

I asked Cayte to stop and she quickly disappeared.

"She is gone," I explained in bated breath, as I could not figure out why she was so curious about her hair. It just didn't make any sense.

Two weeks later I received a call from the manager of the station. He said, "Annette, are you sitting down?" Well, when anyone says that to me I know that something extraordinary is going to be revealed. I quickly sat down.

"I couldn't say anything at the dinner party at the Moss Beach Distillery because what I am about to tell you is a secret. Our talk show hostess had a bout with cancer and lost a great deal of her hair. She had strands of hair woven into her scalp so that it looks like her real hair. This is what Cayte was seeing, I am sure," he said.

"Oh, my God, of course, that's why she kept saying, she had never seen anything like this before! That's incredible," I told him.

He cleared his throat and continued, "I just wanted to give you some feedback and let you know that you were incredible and Cayte proved that she is definitely a real ghost!"

LOYD: Cayte is playful, curious, flirtatious, and even a bit protective—I think.

In September 2008, I had an unusual experience with Cayte.

I was in Pennsylvania to speak at UNIV-CON, a paranormal conference held adjacent to Penn State University. After things were over on the last day of the event, the convention hosts took those speakers who were still around out to dinner, along with several folks who had helped with the convention.

I was seated at a table with several people, including a couple of paranormal investigators I'd gotten to know a bit over the weekend. We were kidding around quite a bit, and perhaps a bit too much for my friendly ghost.

I was holding a menu when suddenly I shuddered visibly, though not in a bad way. I had felt a light touch caressing my neck. The woman to my left saw me shudder and asked what was up. I explained that Cayte was present and what she'd just done.

As I said, we were kidding around more than a little, and she gave me a very "yeah right" look and flicked my head lightly with her forefinger. We laughed.

Not two minutes later, my phone vibrated with a text message. It was Maria Johnston, a Stockton psychic who has worked with me a bit since mid-2008. "Cayte wants to know who that blond is on your left," read the text message.

Well, needless to say *that* got my attention. It was really loud in the place, so I excused myself for a moment and headed outside to call Maria. I got her on the phone and learned that Cayte had popped in on her at home, looking visibly upset. Cayte had said the woman next to me was being very disrespectful and she didn't like it one bit.

I headed back to the table and explained my absence. Folks were a bit blown away, though perhaps also a bit skeptical. Apparently Cayte had bounced from one end of the country where I was, back to California in an instant to speak with Maria Johnston.

In early 2009, Ankhasha Amenti called me in a state of excitement. Both she and Annette had gotten the impression that "Donovan" was not Cayte's married name—remember, Annette had received the name "Elizabeth Claire Donovan." Both had gotten the impression the name might be connected to the boyfriend, who Cayte told Annette was named "Charlie."

Ankhasha thought perhaps the boyfriend was named Charlie Donovan, and started doing some research through recently added-to-the-Internet obituaries. She found one for Charlie Donovan from the 1980s (a few years before my first visit there), and the man's birthdate would have put him in his mid-20s during the time Cayte would have been there. The man's town of residence?

Moss Beach, California.

Ankhasha felt that Cayte would have liked to have been married to Charlie, making her legally "Elizabeth Claire Donovan."

Given the death was twenty-plus years ago, it's a bit tough to track down folks who might know if Charles Donovan was a piano player at Frank's Roadhouse during Prohibition, but we keep hoping to find evidence that confirms or repudiates this.

As to my continued experiences with Cayte, Annette often tells people that I remind Cayte of her boyfriend. And perhaps it's also that I have done so much in the way of investigation and visits there, and put so much into keeping up with her story.

I'm flattered, though sometimes I have to explain that I have my own ghostly stalker (friendly, of course).

Annette and I have returned to the Distillery in 2008 and 2009. One recent visit was in late October, 2009, for a special taping of a three-and-a-half hour radio show for Alice @ 93.7 Radio, a San Francisco station. Before we all sat down to do the show, Annette was definitely in touch with Cayte—I felt her, too—and Cayte did a little stunt for a few of the attendees—she knocked over a chair.

During the taping, Cayte came through easily. Unfortunately, there was so much going on that I felt Cayte didn't get enough air time. Perhaps next time.

Cayte is a wonderful personality. "Cayte, above all the other ghosts that I have seen throughout my life, gives me hope and a sense of calm knowing that there truly is another form of life beyond death," says Annette. "Her laughter, happiness and very feminine ways of flirting, is such a delight, it always brings a smile to my face. Her strong presence is a key for us to another dimension."

Annette and I look forward to every one of our visits to the Moss Beach Distillery. The food is exceptional and the ghost is great too. But I don't have to visit the restaurant to connect with Cayte, since she pops up in my life wherever I am.

Cayte's clearly happy at the Moss Beach Distillery, and that seems to be the key issue for her. As for us, her emotional acceptance of her state and playful attitude makes the place great as a site for continued investigation and monitoring. In the long run, such cases might help us get a better understanding of what a ghost really is and why people keep reporting such encounters.

The Distillery from the side

Will she ever move on? Perhaps if she gets bored.

But, in the meantime, she has the restaurant, the staff, myself and the psychics, attention from locals and tourists, and apparently the time and inclination to travel. More and more mediums report visits from Cayte.

You can bet Annette and I will be hearing from her often.

Directions to the Haunted Locations

The following directions will help you get to the places described in this book, and the map on the next page will get you oriented as to their general locations in the San Francisco area. We hope you have a great time planning and going on your own ghost hunting tour! (Note: We have not included photos or directions for the Mansions Hotel since it is currently a private residence.)

Most of the locations in the book—aside from the Moss Beach Distillery and Alcatraz—can be reached via public transportation in San Francisco. Consult the websites of the locations, or check with BART and MUNI in San Francisco for appropriate route information.

We very heartily recommend Jim Fassbinder's San Francisco Ghost Hunt in Pacific Heights, which starts at the Queen Anne Hotel at 7:00 P.M. Wednesdays through Sundays. For more information, visit sfghosthunt.com, e-mail sfghosthunt@yahoo.com, or call 415-922-5590. The tour is a blast!

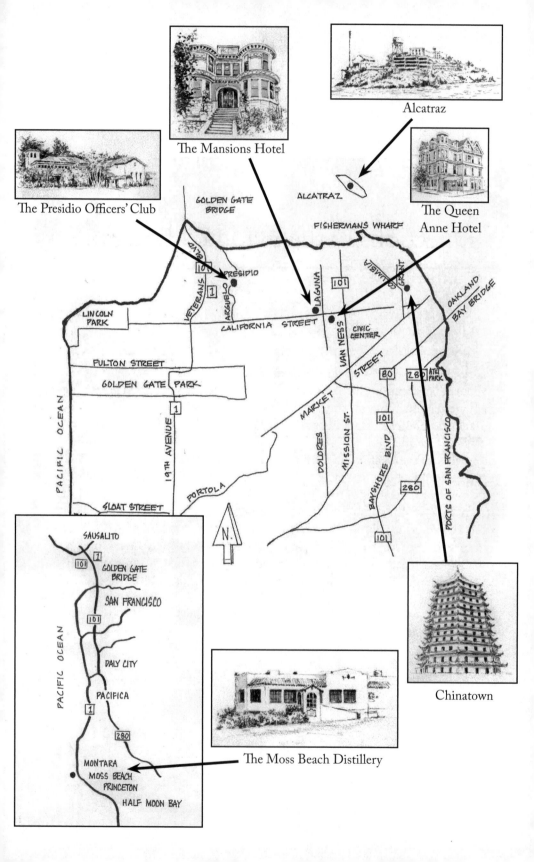

The Mansions Hotel

Alcatraz

The Presidio Officers' Club

The Queen
Anne Hotel

GOLDEN GATE
BRIDGE

ALCATRAZ

FISHERMANS WHARF

PRESIDIO

LAGUNA

GRANT

COLUMBIA

OAKLAND
BAY BRIDGE

LINCOLN
PARK

VETERANS

ARGUELLO

CALIFORNIA STREET

VAN NESS

CIVIC
CENTER

FULTON STREET

GOLDEN GATE PARK

19TH AVENUE

MARKET

DOLORES

MISSION ST.

STREET

BAYSHORE BLVD

80

280

ATER
PARK

PACIFIC OCEAN

PORTOLA

SLOAT STREET

101

101

280

PORTS OF SAN FRANCISCO

N.

SAUSALITO

101

GOLDEN GATE
BRIDGE

SAN FRANCISCO

101

PACIFIC OCEAN

DALY CITY

PACIFICA

1

280

MONTARA
MOSS BEACH
PRINCETON

HALF MOON BAY

Chinatown

The Moss Beach Distillery

Queen Anne Hotel

1590 Sutter Street, San Francisco, CA 94109
Reservations: 1-800-227-3970 Fax: 1-415-775-5212
General Information: 1-415-441-2828
E-mail: stay@queenanne.com

From the South: From Highway 280 North to San Francisco, exit 6th Street (Taylor) to Sutter. Turn left on Sutter. Go nine blocks to 1590 Sutter and Octavia.

From Highway 101 North: Go to the end of the freeway, exit straight onto Octavia. Turn right on Oak. Go two blocks and turn left on Franklin. Continue on Franklin a half-mile and turn left on Sutter. Go two blocks to 1590 Sutter and Octavia.

From the East: Follow signs for San Francisco. Cross over Highway I-80/ The Bay Bridge. Use the first San Francisco exit, Fremont Street. Go five blocks and turn left on Pine. Go fifteen blocks and turn left on Van Ness. Go two blocks and turn right on Sutter. Go three blocks to 1590 Sutter and Octavia.

From the North: From the Golden Gate Bridge (Highway 101), exit on Lombard and continue for thirteen blocks and turn right on Van Ness. Go fifteen blocks and turn right on Sutter Street. Go three blocks to 1590 Sutter and Octavia.

The Presidio Officers' Club

50 Moraga Avenue, San Francisco, CA 94129
General Information: 1-415-561-5444
www.presidio.gov/event/rental/officersclub/

From the Bay Bridge: Take the Fremont Street exit, which will direct you around onto Fremont Street. Cross Market Street and then turn left onto Pine Street. Continue on Pine Street to Franklin Street. Turn right onto Franklin. Turn left onto Lombard Street and stay in the left lane. Following the signs toward the Presidio, use the Lombard Street left hand turn lane (after Broderick Street) to stay on Lombard. Enter the Presidio at the Lombard Gate.

At the second stop sign, turn right onto Presidio Boulevard. At the next stop sign Presidio Boulevard becomes Lincoln Boulevard. Follow Lincoln Boulevard westbound and turn left onto Graham Street. Take Graham Street to the stop sign at Moraga Street. The Officers' Club is straight ahead at the intersection of Graham Street and Moraga Avenue.

North from San Francisco Airport (South Presidio Entrance): From Highway 101, take Highway 380 West to Highway 280 North toward San Francisco. Follow the signs to "Golden Gate Bridge—19th Avenue—Park Presidio." Take a right on California Street. Turn left onto Arguello Boulevard. Enter the Presidio through the Arguello Gate and continue on Arguello to the bottom of the hill. Take a right onto Moraga Avenue. The Officers' Club is immediately on the right.

East from the Lombard Gate (East Presidio Entrance): Enter the Presidio at the Lombard Gate. At the second stop sign, turn right onto Presidio Boulevard. At the next stop sign, Presidio Boulevard becomes Lincoln Boulevard. Follow Lincoln Boulevard westbound and turn left onto Graham Street. Take Graham Street to the stop sign at Moraga Street. The Officers' Club is at the intersection of Moraga Avenue and Graham Street.

From the Marina Gate (Northeast Presidio Entrance): Follow Mason Street west. Turn left onto Halleck Street. Take Halleck Street to the stop sign and turn right onto Lincoln Boulevard. Turn left onto Graham Street. Take Graham Street to the stop sign at Moraga Street. The Officers' Club is straight ahead at the intersection of Graham Street and Moraga Avenue.

South from the Golden Gate Bridge (Northwest Presidio Entrance): Be sure to be in the far right toll lane. From the toll plaza, take the very first right (at the bus stop) onto Merchant Avenue. Merchant Avenue ends at Lincoln Boulevard. Turn left onto Lincoln Boulevard and follow Lincoln Boulevard east to the Main Post. Lincoln will become Sheridan as you enter the Main Post near the National Cemetery. Proceed straight on Sheridan crossing Montgomery Street at the stop sign. Turn right onto Graham Street. Take Graham Street to the stop sign at Moraga Street. The Officers' Club is straight ahead at the intersection of Graham Street and Moraga Avenue.

From the 25th Avenue Gate/El Camino Del Mar (Southwest Presidio Entrance): Once in the Presidio, El Camino del Mar becomes Lincoln Boulevard. Follow Lincoln Boulevard north and then east to the Main Post. Lincoln will become Sheridan as you enter the Main Post near the National Cemetery. Proceed straight on Sheridan crossing Montgomery Street at the stop sign. Turn right onto Graham Street. Take Graham Street to the stop sign at Moraga Avenue. The Officers' Club is at the intersection of Moraga Avenue and Graham Street.

From the Presidio Boulevard Gate (Southeast Presidio Entrance): Follow Presidio Boulevard down the hill. At the first stop sign, proceed straight. At the second stop sign, Presidio Boulevard becomes Lincoln Boulevard. After this second stop sign, continue on Lincoln Boulevard westbound and turn left onto Graham Street. Take Graham Street to the stop sign at Moraga Avenue. The Officers' Club is straight ahead at the intersection of Graham Street and Moraga Avenue.

From the Arguello Gate (South Presidio Entrance): Follow Arguello Boulevard downhill to the first stop sign. Turn right onto Moraga Avenue. The Officers' Club is immediately on the right.

San Francisco Chinatown

Parking isn't just scarce here, it's almost non-existent. The Portsmouth Square Garage on Kearny is hard to get to: You have to drive all the way around the block, often waiting in a slow-moving line, but if you have patience this will work well. Sometimes the St. Mary's Square Garage on California may be a better bet. On weekends, you can park your car at The Golden Gateway Garage (250 Clay Street between Front and Davis) and take a free shuttle from there. If you spend at least $3.00 with a merchant, you can get validation for a reduced parking rate.

On foot from Union Square, take Geary, Maiden Lane, or Post east one block to Grant Avenue and go north to the Chinatown gate. If you're coming from North Beach, just cross Columbus onto Grant and you're there. We suggest that anyone walking in San Francisco wear comfortable shoes, an extra layer of warm clothing, hats, visors, and sunglasses. The weather can be sunny but cool.

If you're visiting Union Square or North Beach on the same day, you can also park there and walk to Chinatown.

For an added treat you, can get there on San Francisco's cable cars, which are the last of their kind in the world and are utterly fun and charming. The California line stops at California and Grant, or you can get off the Powell line at California and walk three blocks to Grant.

We highly recommend San Francisco Chinatown Ghost Tours, with Cynthia Yee. They can be reached a 1-415-793-1183 or 1-877-887-3373, or at info@sfchinatownghosttours.com.

Alcatraz

AlcatrazCruises.com

Take snacks and drinks with you, as there is no food sold on the island. Be sure to dress warmly, even in the summer. Allow at least three hours for the round trip boat ride and tour on the island. Since Alcatraz is very popular, it's advisable to buy your tickets about ninety days ahead of your trip (alcatrazcruises.com). You can also purchase tickets at the Hornblower Alcatraz Landing Ticket office at Pier 33. The Early Bird tour leaves at 9 A.M. and the ferries leave every half-hour until 2 P.M. Evening tours are available from Thursday through Monday and are definitely more spooky. Alcatraz is closed on Thanksgiving, Christmas, and New Year's Day (and, rarely, due to extreme weather).

Parking: On-street parking in the area the ferry departs from can be difficult to find, especially during peak summer visitation season. Plus, nearly every street space has a parking meter with a time limit insufficient for an Alcatraz visit. An "Accessibility Drop Off Zone" is located at the entrance to Alcatraz Cruises—Pier 33 for visitors with special needs arriving by automobile. There are fifteen commercial lots within a five-block radius of the Alcatraz Cruises, with a total of more than 3,000 parking spaces. But, we recommend you use public transportation if at all possible. Prices for parking in this area can vary greatly: from as little as $8.00 to $10.00 for all day, to as high as $6.00 an hour. As a visit to Alcatraz can easily take two to three hours (or more), it can be worthwhile to shop around for parking.

Public Transportation: When in San Francisco, public transportation is the best way to get around. The Muni F Line runs along Market Street (east), then turns north on The Embarcadero and runs right past the ferry terminal (on your right) and on through Fisherman's Wharf.

The Moss Beach Distillery

140 Beach Way, Moss Beach, California 94038
1-650-728-5595 www.MossBeachDistillery.com

The Distillery is located on the Pacific Ocean in an area called the San Mateo County Coastside. The restaurant is a few blocks off of Highway 1, twenty-five miles south of San Francisco, between Pacifica and Half Moon Bay. Driving times are approximately twenty minutes west of San Mateo, thirty-five minutes south of San Francisco, and forty-five minutes from the East and South Bay.

From San Francisco: Take 101 South to 280 South. Exit at Highway 1 South, Pacifica, and continue approximately thirteen miles. Look for the big sign for the Distillery as you enter Moss Beach. Turn right at Cypress Avenue and follow the signs to the restaurant. (Turn right at Marine Boulevard, turn left at Beach Way.)

From the South: Take 101 North or 280 North to Highway 92 West, towards Half Moon Bay. Once in Half Moon Bay, turn right on Highway 1 North. Go approximately six miles. Look for the big sign for the Distillery as you enter Moss Beach. Turn right at Cypress Avenue and follow the signs to the restaurant. (Turn right at Marine Boulevard, turn left at Beach Way.)

From the East: Take Highway 92 West, towards Half Moon Bay. Once in Half Moon Bay, turn right on Highway 1 North. Go approximately six miles. Look for the big sign for the Distillery as you enter Moss Beach. Turn right at Cypress Avenue and follow the signs to the restaurant. (Turn right at Marine Boulevard, turn Left at Beach Way.)

Ghost Hunting Do's and Don'ts

Are you ready to do a bit of ghost hunting? Before you take the field and have your own ghostly encounters, let me give you a few pointers to get help you out. Trust me—these were learned through slow, hard experience!

—Loyd Auerbach

What to Do

Do learn some basics of what parapsychologists and psychical researchers have learned about apparitions, hauntings and poltergeists.

Do learn how to actually use the technology/equipment. Learn what the devices are designed to detect (it's not ghosts), and learn the limitations of the sensors. Learn about false readings. Learn what sorts of things can give you unusual (non-paranormal) images on film and digital media when taking photos and video. Learn what sorts of things might cause unusual sounds on audiotape.

Do learn interviewing skills so you can question the witnesses appropriately.

Do look for non-paranormal explanations for both the overall case you investigate and the individual events reported by the witnesses. Question everything.

Do realize that some explanations can be rather bizarre without being paranormal. Look for unusual and rarely seen "normal" explanations.

Do take note of people's experiences and perceptions. Consider working with psychics or sensitives, as long as they are "team players" and are willing to be questioned about what they experience (in other words, only work with psychics who can admit they are not always right).

Do pay attention to what you experience yourself, but always look for alternative explanations.

Do take special note of instances when the technology *and* the humans are perceiving something out of the ordinary at the same time.

Do combine all data from technology with the experiential reports of the witnesses and any perceptions of psychics/sensitives, your teammates, and yourself. Do learn how to properly correlate data from the tech to the witness experiences and reported phenomena.

Do ask lots of questions.

Do respect the people in the location you investigate. Put their needs for resolution of the situation above your need to "get something." Do be helpful to people beyond simply validating their experiences.

What *Not* to Do

Don't go to any location without obtaining full permission from the owner/person(s) leasing or renting and inhabitants. Don't "investigate" a public location (restaurant, museum, hotel) without permission, and don't react badly to a "no thank you," especially where an operating business is concerned.

Don't go alone. This is to protect you from possible threats from the living, not the dead. Such threats might be a result of a witness/client being psychologically disturbed (rather than having a real paranormal experience). In addition, this protects you from possible legal problems should the clients decide they don't like the way you're handling their situation and accuse you of misconduct.

Don't jump to conclusions.

Don't believe technology over human perceptions (*do* remember that none of the tech has been designed to detect "ghosts," no matter what the advertising literature for the tech says).

Don't scare people with pronouncements of ghosts unless a) you're sure of what's going on and b) they can handle such news.

Don't scare them with pronouncements of "demons" or "malevolent entities"—better to couch the terminology as "harmful" or "potentially dangerous," *if* that's your assessment (and be careful with this as well). You'll only increase their fear level.

Don't leave the situation and the people without some kind of resolution or referral for further help.

Don't leave without giving them good information about psychic phenomena.

Don't involve the media without first discussing with the people involved all that the media encompasses. Get their full permission!

Don't show up to a case wearing team shirts/jackets/colors/logos and don't have signs proclaiming your activity on your vehicles for any case where confidentiality and privacy has been promised.

Paranormal Investigation Checklist

1) Ask as many questions as possible before going on the investigation.

2) Confirm that the phenomena/experiences are still going on, that there is more than one witness, and that there's a need to investigate at all.

3) Explore normal causes for the reported phenomena before going.

4) Don't go alone to any location other than a public venue (restaurant, museum, etc.). You don't need a full team, but have at least one person accompany you.

5) Gather what equipment you think you may need, especially recording devices (camera, tape recorder, video camera, paper and pen).

6) Avoid publicity and debunkers. (Note: Finding alternative explanations is not debunking. It's Science)

7) Make sure all witnesses can either be interviewed on site or are otherwise available. Also make sure non-witness residents of the place are available for interview.

8) Ask lots of questions. Conduct in-depth interviews.

9) Look for normal explanations for each of the individual incidents and for the overall case.

10) Look for relationships between the people and the events.

11) Gather data with detection devices and psychics/intuitives. Try the characteristics checklist (see www.mindreader.com/opi.htm).

12) Observe! Ask more questions and observe some more!

13) Assess and discuss the data gathered (from interviews, detectors, sensitives and investigators' opinions) to make an assessment.

14) Decide what to do next: further visits, education, resolution techniques, or a combination (or nothing at all). Then do it!

15) Write up a report—if for no other reason, so that you can keep track of cases.

Loyd Auerbach

Loyd Auerbach is well-known to the public as a leading expert on Ghosts and Psychic Experience. With a Master's degree in Parapsychology, he is Director of the Office of Paranormal Investigations, a Professor at JFK University, and creator and Instructor of the Certificate Program in Parapsychological Studies at HCH Institute, available both in California and for distance learning. In late 2010, he was appointed to the faculty of Atlantic University of Virginia Beach, Virginia, to help develop and teach online courses for the upcoming M.A. in Parapsychology Program.

He is a member of the Advisory Boards of both the Rhine Research Center and the Windbridge Institute, and the Scientific Advisory Board of the Forever Family Foundation. He was a Consulting Editor and columnist for *FATE* magazine from 1991–2004.

Auerbach is the author of seven books on the Paranormal, including *A Paranormal Casebook: Ghost Hunting in the New Millennium* (Atriad Press, 2005), *Hauntings & Poltergeists: A Ghost Hunter's Guide* (Ronin Publishing, 2004) and *Ghost Hunting: How to Investigate the Paranormal* (Ronin, 2004).

He is a professional mentalist and psychic entertainer, performing as Professor Paranormal—a title that follows him into his more serious work. He is a past President of the Psychic Entertainers Association (and currently on the Board of Directors).

He has appeared in hundreds of radio and print interviews, and well over 100 national and local TV shows including *The View, Larry King Live, The Oprah Winfrey Show, Criss Angel: Mindfreak, Sightings, In Search Of, The Today Show, Unsolved Mysteries, Late Night with David Letterman,* and frequently on A&E, the History Channel, the Travel Channel, the Syfy Channel, the Discovery Channel and the Learning Channel.

Visit his Paranormal Network website at **www.MindReader.com**.

As of 2010, after taking a professional chocolatier course, he has branched out with his own chocolate products and business. Visit **www.HauntedByChocolate.com** for more information. He lives with his wife and three cats outside of San Francisco.

Annette Martin

The first psychic to ever testify as an expert witness in a murder trial, **Annette Martin** first experienced what she calls the "Gift of the White Light" at age 7. Over the years she realized that it was a gift from God and that it was her mission in this life to learn how to use its awesome power to help people.

Martin was living in Hong Kong when she began providing professional medical readings, and it was then that Edgar Cayce first appeared to her. Cayce politely asked that she remain calm and told her he would help her with her health readings. Over the ensuing years Cayce has been mystically, lovingly and helpfully by her side during thousands of sessions.

During a difficult time in his life, song writer John Denver learned of Martin and requested a reading. Denver, an aviation buff, told her he had a desire to go into outer space, perhaps on one of NASA's space shuttles. Annette said she didn't see that, but she did see him flying a small craft that would tumble down and crash into the ocean. Fifteen years later Denver died when he lost control of a small experimental plane he was flying and crashed into the ocean off of Pacific Grove, California.

Martin has used her psychic talents to crack murder cases, locate missing persons, solve medical mysteries that puzzled expert doctors, make verified predictions for individuals, and help put criminals in jail. Annette has appeared on the Biography Channel's *Psychic Investigators*, *Coast to Coast with George Noory*, *Good Morning America*, Court TV's *Psychic Detective*, *Entertainment Tonight*, *The Nancy Grace Show*, *The Catherine Cryer Show*, *48 Hours*, *The Montel Williams Show* and hundreds of radio appearances and print interviews.

Annette has taught hundreds of students and is the author of *Discovering Your Psychic World*, about learning how to develop your intuition (Artistic Visions, 1994), *Peaceful White Light Meditation* CDs (Artistic Visions, 1994), and the children's story *Annie Sunshine and the White Owl of the Cedars* (Artistic Visions, 1998).

Martin's amazing life story and psychic abilities were documented in *The Gift of the White Light*, a biography by James N. Frey (Quill Driver Books, 2008). Martin is the director of Closure4U Investigations (**www.Closure4u.com**), a detective agency using traditional and psychic investigation techniques to investigate cases involving homicide, missing persons, grand theft, arson and industrial espionage.

Learn more about amazing psychic Annette Martin by reading....

Gift of the White Light
the Strange and Wonderful Story of
Annette Martin, Psychic

a biography by James N. Frey

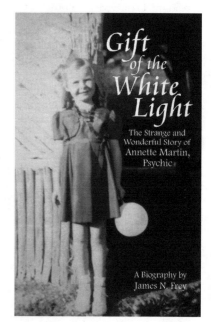